cybergrrl!

A WOMAN'S GUIDE TO THE WORLD WIDE WEB

ALIZA SHERMAN

BALLANTINE BOOKS • NEW YORK

cybergrrl!

A WOMAN'S GUIDE TO THE WORLD WIDE WEB

A Ballantine Book
Published by The Ballantine Publishing Group

Copyright © 1998 by Aliza Sherman

All rights reserved under International and Pan-American Copyright Conventions. Published in the United States by The Ballantine Publishing Group, a division of Random House, Inc., New York, and simultaneously in Canada by Random House of Canada Limited, Toronto.

 CYBERGRRL and WEBGRRLS are trademarks of Cybergrrl, Inc., and are used with permission.

http://www. randomhouse.com

Library of Congress Catalog Card Number: 97-94354

ISBN: 0-345-42382-8

Cover design by Barbara Leff
Cover art © L Sherman/1997 Cybergrrl, Inc.
Book design by Fritz Metsch

Manufactured in the United States of America

First Edition: February 1998

10 9 8 7 6 5 4

A HEARTFELT, ONGOING THANKS TO:

my business partner, the staff at Cybergrrl, Inc., and all Webgrrls around the world—all of whom have contributed directly or indirectly to helping women and girls become technologically savvy.

A SPECIAL THANKS TO:

my very cool editor, Amy Scheibe, and other awesome Ballantineites including Ellen Archer, Jennifer Richards, Barbara Leff, and Cindy Berman; the most excellent research assistant Julie Roth; my additional researchers, AnnMarie Pennola, Michelle Chen, and Evelyn Chan; and my special editors—Alison Berke, my sister Leah, Mom, Dad, and Ese.

If it weren't for the Internet, you wouldn't be reading this book. I honestly believe I wouldn't even have the opportunity to publish this book if I hadn't gone online. Being online helped me get exposure for my writing and my work. I want women and girls to benefit from technology just as I have and as many other women do every day. Getting online is a great way to start.

Contents

Appendixes

cybergrrl!

A WOMAN'S GUIDE TO THE WORLD WIDE WEB

Introduction

Cybergrrl says . . .
   If you think the Internet and the World Wide Web . . .

   is too hard
   is too expensive
   is too dangerous
   offers you nothing professionally
   offers you nothing personally

then think again.

- Eva Shaderowfsky, fifty-nine, discovered the Internet when she was bedridden with chronic fatigue syndrome. Being online is her connection to the world.
- Francine Gutwilik, thirty-two, publishes a complete daily menu plan online every week at her *Yummyzine* website for working moms like herself, including a shopping list of ingredients that can be printed out and brought along to the grocery store.
- Amy Ormond, twenty-eight, started a mail-order business selling feminine products to busy women. She publicizes her business, The Women's Pharmacy, on her website and publishes a quarterly "magazine" online, *BodyShock,* that addresses the unique health concerns of girls.
- Paige Braddock, twenty-seven, publishes her humorous cartoon just for women, "See Jane," and even sells promotional T-shirts and mugs online.
- Aliza Sherman (me), thirty, found a community of women online who inspired her to build her own website and publish her own writing on the Web. That led her to launch the cartoon character "Cybergrrl," created to be "Your Guide to Going Online," and to start her own business building websites for companies and nonprofit organizations.

Women are online in force, hooking up personally, finding new opportunities professionally, "networking" with women all over the world. If you go online, you can find hundreds of communities of women worldwide discussing everything from parenting to starting a business to sewing to website design. You can meet women who are artists, secretaries, computer programmers, and moms just by visiting their personal websites. You can get answers to almost any question you might have, from career advice to cooking tips to information on rare health disorders.

We all overcame the barriers that seem to keep many women from going online. And if you follow our example, you'll discover how useful a tool the Internet (the Net) and the World Wide Web (the Web) can be both professionally and personally.

Cybergrrl will show you:

- Easy ways to get online that don't cost a fortune
- Real examples of how the Internet has changed women's lives, and can change yours, too
- The truth about online stalking, harassment, and pornography
- How to find useful information online, both professional (great job, career, and business resources) and personal (resources about health, family, home, and more)
- Profiles of women who are online and loving it

How to Use This Book

If you read this book cover to cover, you'll find some things repeated throughout. I do this not only to reinforce them and remind you, but also so, if you choose to skip around from chapter to chapter, you can get the background information you need.

Also, whenever I mention a new term or concept, it will be in bold with a brief explanation, but you can also check the Glossary in the back for a definition.

I try to include as many real-life examples of the different things I talk about, because it's important to know that you are not alone in what you are going through as you try to learn about getting online.

And at the end of every chapter, I will sum up some of the most important points covered to give you a quick reference section. There is a lot of information in here, but these features will make it easy to understand and access what you need to know!

Open your mind to the possibilities and opportunities going online can bring to your job, your home, and your everyday life. Let Cybergrrl show you how easy it is to get online and how to get the most out of being there!

Who Is Cybergrrl?

Cybergrrl is my online alter ego, the champion of women and girls online. I first created her when I was building my own personal website. But before I get to that, you probably want to know how I learned about the Internet and the World Wide Web in the first place.

The "techie" part of my story may sound familiar to some of you and completely alien to others, so if you feel as if you're getting in over your head, just skip to the cross-references I've indicated to get yourself up to speed.

I always say "I'm not a techie," but I've certainly learned a great deal about computers and the Internet in a few short years. I've never taken a computer class, and I was never exposed to computers in school, not even in college. I'm part of the generation who just missed computers in schools, but I was definitely part of the generation of girls who were taught to type so they'd have a good skill to "fall back on." I learned to type in the ninth grade, did all my high school and college papers on an electric typewriter, and became a secretary out of college.

It was while I was a secretary that I first learned about computers. I was told by the temp agency I was with that I could earn more money if I had computer skills. A few extra dollars an hour was motivation enough to get someone to show me how to use a word processor. Honestly, as a writer, I thought the moment I touched the computer, it would zap any creativity I had. Something about the cold, plastic machine and glaring screen seemed really scary to me. But once I learned how to turn the thing on, open a program, type a letter, save it, and print it, I was hooked.

I bought my first computer in 1989, using the money I made from selling my car when I moved to New York City. The only reason I bought it was for word processing—I had dreams of being a writer. I bought the computer simply to type my manuscripts, which I hoped to find the courage to submit.

A neighbor helped me pick out the right computer (one I could afford) and showed me how to set it up and use it. I bought an Amstrad 1640, which probably doesn't mean much to anyone now, but it was an off-white computer with a big black screen, a keyboard, a mouse, and two big floppy disk drives.

Then my neighbor showed me how to "go online." He put a disk into the floppy drive which opened a software program that appeared on the screen. Then he entered a phone number into the program; suddenly I heard a dial tone and my computer began dialing the number. I waited in anticipation.

Then text automatically scrolled up the screen welcoming me, and a numbered list appeared in the middle of the screen with choices I could make, such as:

```
Welcome. Choose one of the following:
1. Go to posting boards
2. Go to games
3. About this service
4. Edit your profile
```

I soon learned that I was connecting to a local bulletin board system (BBS), which was a computer, probably in someone's home, that I could connect to with my own computer through my phone line. For me, "going online" meant playing word games like Hangman and reading messages that other people had left behind on "posting boards" (see Chapter 7). A posting board looked something like this on my computer screen:

```
Username Date      Subject                    Time
johndoe  11/2/89   Hello everyone             12:30am
bob      11/2/89   Read any good books?       12:55am
alan     11/2/89   RE: Read any good books?   2:15am
scruffy  11/3/89   RE: Read any good books?   5:50am
happy    11/4/89   What's up?                 2:20am
```

I would simply select the message I wanted to read by putting my cursor on it and hitting Return; the message would then appear on the screen. All I had to do was read instructions and information and type in some "commands" or hit Return to get around these computer systems.

Then one day I was connected to a BBS and I got an "instant message." I was minding my own business and playing a game when suddenly a message flashed on the screen that said, "Do you want to talk?" I jumped out of my chair, looked around my apartment, and actually thought the computer was talking to me (okay, so maybe I read a lot of science fiction). Until that moment, I had never actually understood that other people were connected to the same computer as I, and that we could communicate with one another. Going online suddenly made sense: I could communicate with other people, a great thing for any writer to discover.

Joining Online Services

Over the Christmas holidays of 1991 I decided to expand my online horizons and signed up for accounts with three online services—companies that provide access to their computers so users can participate in all sorts of activities, including reading things, researching information, and communicating with other people. I tried a small national service called Women's Wire (no longer in existence), which was exclusively by and for women, and a large commercial online service called America Online, as well as a local, text-only service called ECHO (East Coast Hangout).

I quickly began using this new "online thing" to write,

publish, and build resources for other women. How did I do that? I called the then-president of Women's Wire in San Francisco, Ellen Pack, and asked if I could build a "forum" on her online service. A forum on this particular service was a collection of information on a specific topic with "posting boards" (also called message boards or bulletin boards), a place where other people could comment about the topic and start online "conversations."

When you connected to Women's Wire, you would see, on your computer screen, a bunch of neatly arranged folders, like the icons on computers with Windows or the folders of a Macintosh computer. Each folder had a different name to convey the topic of discussion, such as Politics, Environment, Health, and Welcome Wagon. When you double-clicked on a folder, you found more folders inside as well as files you could read that might be articles or, if you were in the posting board area, posts from other people.

Picture This: To visualize the concept of a posting board, imagine an actual bulletin board where people can tack messages each day and other people can stop by the board, read the messages, and tack on their own. Some of the messages might be questions for which people want answers, while others are stories or interesting information pertaining to the common topic. With an online posting board, the messages may be electronic but the concept is the same.

When you first enter a posting board area, you see lines of text on your computer screen that usually include someone's name or nickname, the date and time, and the subject of the post, each line representing one post. You have to open the post (the process is slightly different with each service) before you can read it. You can usually tell what a post is about according to its subject.

Building Things Online

As the executive director of a domestic violence awareness group, I had accumulated a lot of valuable information. This is what I wanted to "put online." To do this, I electronically sent the documents of information to the Women's Wire system, and they remained in one place under the name Safety Net, which became a forum on issues of violence against women. I thought the topic of domestic violence was important, and I believed that women online would appreciate a place to go to find out about this sensitive issue that greatly affects the lives of women. The forum helped a lot of women talk about their experiences and learn how they could help themselves and other women.

America Online was a much larger service than Women's Wire, so I wasn't able to pick up the phone and call the president. On America Online (AOL), I went into a chatroom, which is a place on the service where people post messages to one another that instantly appear on the computer screen and where conversations are held, like in a telephone call, but where everyone types instead of speaks. I was amazed at this newfound use for my computer—who knew a computer could connect me to other people just to "talk"?

On both of these services, I also discovered how easy it was to send email—electronic mail—and I sent messages to people all over the world. On AOL, I started sending "group emails," sending email to women on the service to share information and to network with one another. I called it The Women's List.

Discovering the Web

I learned about the World Wide Web in November 1994. I had fled New York City for Santa Fe, New Mexico, after a friend and I were held up at gunpoint. Although we managed to escape unharmed and all three of the guys were caught, I was really shaken up and decided to visit my sister out west to recover.

While looking through a local art magazine, I saw an ad that said "Discover the World Wide Web." I had no idea what the World Wide Web was, but I saw an email address in the ad. I knew what email was, so I quickly went online and sent an email to the address. I got a reply from a man who called himself a Web designer, who invited me to take a class to learn the basics of building a website. I didn't understand what he meant by a "website," so he and his girlfriend invited me to their house to show me "the Web." Once I saw websites, the rest of the Internet suddenly seemed boring.

That week I took a one-hour, $10 class on the basics of building websites (the only computer class I've ever taken), and the whole world opened up to me. Think of a website as a database of information that people can access online and that can contain text, images, and other media—like sound and video (that's what is meant by the term *multimedia*)—instead of just text. By building my own website, I could self-publish on the Internet and make my writing available to anyone anywhere in the world who went online. I didn't have to ask anyone's permission or follow anyone's rules. This was an exciting idea.

In January 1995, I debuted my first website, The Web According to Cybergrrl. Instead of putting a photograph of myself on the site, which many people were doing, I drew a cartoon character instead and called her Cybergrrl. Her name combined "cyber" referring to "cyberspace," which was a term being used for the undefined "space" created by the networked computers of the Internet, and "grrl" to represent the "strong version of girl" or "girl with attitude," as I like to say since "girl" sounded too young.

Cybergrrl has quickly become the superheroine of the Internet and "Your Guide to Going Online." She champions getting more women and girls online to make sure they aren't left behind in our increasingly technical workplace and world.

I'm living proof that you don't have to be a techie or computer whiz to benefit from the Internet. Going online isn't really about computers; it's about communication as well as making connections to both information and people. And making connections can help you in many aspects of your life—personally *and* professionally. Cybergrrl says . . . Get online!

part one

GETTING STARTED ONLINE—THE NUTS AND BOLTS

Chapter 1   What Is the Internet?

Beware of Techie Types!

In my introduction, I used a few techie terms, but I tried to explain what everything means because some of these words and concepts might be new to you.

Before you begin flipping pages and convincing yourself that you'll never understand the Internet, let me assure you right now that there's nothing about the Internet that you don't already understand, you just haven't had it explained to you in a way that makes sense. Often, someone more technically inclined tries to introduce you to the "wonders of going online," and proceeds to throw around all kinds of confusing terms like 28.8 bps modems, TCP/IP, SLIP, or PPP connections and a lot of other alphabet soup that you don't really need to know right away.

Don't despair! Techie types are not always capable of putting things into everyday language, so it's not your fault when your eyes glaze over. Also, learning exactly what those letters and words stand for won't change your life or the world, you just need to relate to what they mean. There are easy ways to learn and understand what those terms represent so you can buy the right computer with confidence or subscribe to an online service to get the cheapest and most direct access to go online.

My goal is to explain these terms in a way that makes sense and also to show how going online can be easy, useful, and even fun.

So What Is the Internet, Really?

What is the Internet? I like to say that the Internet is a loose, worldwide **network** of computers serving up **databases**, or "collections," of information to the public via **servers**. And a server is just another word for computer—it's a computer that is connected to the Internet twenty-four hours a day, seven days a week. If you work in an office, you might already know about networks. With the Internet, think about the concept of connecting computers and sharing information as being similar to the connected computers in your office, but on a global scale.

Maybe you've heard the term *information superhighway*? Well, if you aren't able to visualize what it means, that's because it doesn't give you the whole picture. If you're not familiar with computer networks in offices and can't figure out what a highway has to do with anything, let's try an analogy:

Picture This: The Internet is like a lot of small towns connected by roads and highways. In the towns are libraries, hospitals, government offices, stores, office buildings, and, of course, houses. You could leave your house, get into your car, and drive to the local library to read or check out a book, or you could go to the store to buy something or to a government office to get a copy of a document.

If the Internet is like an electronic version of towns and roads, then imagine that you can use your computer to travel on electronic roads—phone lines—and go to these same kinds of places using your computer. You can then connect to these places and get similar information, services, or products that you'd get in the real world, only you're not leaving home. This is one of the conveniences of the Internet.

A network on the Internet is like a network of roads connecting buildings in a town and highways connecting one town to another. On the Internet, this network is actually made up of hundreds of thousands of computers or servers "networked" together to share information. You could say the servers are "internetworked," which can be shortened to the "Internet." Clever, aren't they?

In reality, you can't see all of the connections that link up all the servers on the Internet the way you can see roads and highways. Most of the servers around the world that are "connected" to the Internet are communicating with one another by talking the same computer language.

Picture This: Information travels over the phone lines—the electronic roads—in the same way we drive on roads in a car. We all have to follow certain rules so we can get through the traffic to our destination. And so does electronic information traveling from computer to computer.

Now think of this vast, loose network of computers or servers that are all talking the same language, and imagine that you can connect to them through your own home or office computer (see Chapter 3 for how to do it). When you connect to the Internet, your computer "talks" to another computer, and when a connection is made, you are able to access the contents of the **hard drives** or "storage spaces" on those other computers.

Picture This: Going back to the buildings, roads, and towns idea, now think of your home as a representation of your computer. Your computer, like your home, is made up of rooms where you can do things and other rooms where you can store things. The hard drive of your computer is like a room where you can store things. You have the things organized in certain ways—like boxes or files in a filing cabinet. You can access these things by opening the door and entering the room.

A hard drive is the part of your computer where information is stored. When you are connected to, or "on," the Internet, you are connecting to other computers and getting into parts of their hard drives. How can you do this?

Well, in your house, other people can enter all the rooms if they are part of your family or sharing your living space. That's like people sharing your computer and accessing your files. There might also be rooms that are locked and only you have the key. This is the same thing as putting a password on your computer or on a file in your computer so no one else can get in.

You usually don't allow total strangers to enter your house or certain rooms in your house, but can invite people to enter your house and to go into these rooms. Likewise, you can go next door and enter your neighbor's house if you are invited. Maybe your neighbor is having a garage sale, and total strangers are entering a part of his house and rummaging through his things. And by going next door, you've expanded your access to things, simply by entering his garage.

When you connect to the Internet with your computer, and then connect to another computer or server, not only are you able to access the contents of your own computer—your files, documents, and all of your information—but you are also able to move through parts of the hard drives or "rooms" of other computers and access files that they make available to you in their special public collections of information or databases. Think of the garage they've opened up for you as a store you can go to or the public library where you can look around.

A database is simply a collection of information or **data** that is organized in a special way to make it easier for you and other people to gain access.

Picture This: A good example of an actual database on the Internet is an electronic phone directory. When you connect to an electronic Yellow Pages, for example, you can then search the database by someone's name, address, the city or state he or she lives in, or the phone number.

The names and numbers in the directory are stored electronically as a collection of data or database in a computer somewhere, say the phone company. If you are connected to the phone company's computer through the Internet, and can access its public storage room of information, then you can use its Yellow Pages database to search for names, numbers, and addresses.

Why Can We Access Other People's Computers?

When the Internet was first developed, its main purpose was to allow military and government agencies to communicate and exchange information they had on their vast computer systems in a fast and efficient way. Once the Internet became accessible to the general public, people set up servers on the Internet and arranged databases or rooms on their computer hard drives that other people could access to communicate, to collaborate, or just to share information.

Lexis-Nexis is an example of a special computer system set up for a particular group of people. Lexis, the first commercial, full-text legal information service, was created in 1973 to help legal professionals research the law more efficiently. Today, hundreds of thousands of professionals worldwide—including lawyers, accountants, financial analysts, journalists, marketers, and information specialists—perform an estimated 300,000 searches a day on Lexis and its companion Nexis®, a news and information service that was started in 1979. Both of these are fee-based services with special computer systems.

Keep in mind that not all information on servers is available to the public. Some servers, such as a bank's computers, are protected with a password so people can access it only if they have an account with the bank. Other servers, such as those at the Pentagon, have an array of passwords and barriers to entry to protect access from anyone except top military personnel. So just because a computer is connected to the Internet doesn't mean you can get into it—unless, of course, you're a hacker and somehow manage to break in!

Don't worry about hackers breaking into your personal computer if you connect to the Internet. For that to happen, they would need to know the telephone number to the phone line connecting your computer to the Internet, then your computer needs to be powered on at all times, and they also need the password for your computer to access the files.

The chance of a random hacker pinpointing your personal computer is very slim, and the thought of breaking in to get your personal files does not present an interesting challenge to them. Hackers usually target large corporate or government computer systems and break in just to show they can.

Let's Not Talk Tech, Let's Talk Tools

In writing this book, my biggest challenge was to talk about the things you need in order to get online without all the mumbo jumbo lingo.

Four main things are needed for you to go online:

a computer with a modem
the right software
a phone line
an account with an online service provider

If you have all of these things, you can skip the rest of this chapter and go directly to Chapter 3 to find out how to get online. But if you're just now contemplating buying a computer, or you have a computer and need to know how to adapt it for online access, then Chapter 2 is for you.

Don't feel that you have to memorize all the information in this chapter. Use this book like the pocket language dictionary you take with you when you travel, or the lists you take to the grocery store. Since *Cybergrrl!* fits into your backpack or pocketbook, it's easy to take it with you when you're shopping for your computer! Let's face it: Going to a computer store can be as alien as going to a foreign country, and having a guide with you can be very helpful.

Wrapup

The Internet is a loose network of computers around the world serving up databases or collections of information to the public using "servers." A server is just another word for computer—it's a computer that is connected to the Internet, the worldwide network, twenty-four hours a day, seven days a week.

The Internet is like a lot of small towns connected together by roads and highways. In the towns are libraries, hospitals, government offices, stores, office buildings, and, of course, houses.

A network on the Internet is like a network of roads connecting buildings in a town and highways connecting towns to one another. This network is actually made up of hundreds of thousands of computers or servers "networked" together to share information.

When you connect to the Internet, your computer "talks" to another computer, and when a connection is made, you are able to access the contents of the hard drives of those other computers.

Now that we've reviewed the concepts of the Internet, let's talk about the things you need to connect to it.

Chapter 2   Nuts and Bolts: Getting the Things You Need

Item #1: Hardware

Think of **hardware** as the computer stuff you can touch and feel—the tangible objects or things. If you go back to the house as a visual image for a computer, then the hardware are the walls that make up the rooms and enclose the house itself, the doors, the windows, even the electrical wiring.

On a computer, the hardware includes:

1. The **CPU (central processing unit)**—usually the box you can lay flat on a desk or stand vertically on a desk or on the floor

In a way, you can think of the CPU as the brain of the computer. If you had a system that kept track of all the electrical activity within your house, what lights were on or which appliances were running, that would be like the brain of your house. The processing of information in your computer is like the electrical activity throughout your house and the CPU keeps track of it all.

2. The **monitor**—usually a separate unit that sits on top of your desk or on top of the CPU and resembles a television screen

Think of the monitor as a window of your house. You can view the contents of the house through this window, and in a sense you can view the contents of your computer through the monitor.

3. The **cables** and any **peripherals** or attachments

The cables and peripherals are like the wiring in your house. On a computer, they connect the different parts of your computer together if the pieces are separate, and they connect your computer to the phone line, other computers, a printer, a scanner, or other attachments that perform a function that the computer alone cannot do. Other very common peripherals that are connected to your computer by cables are a keyboard for typing and a mouse to select objects on the screen and activate programs.

Some computers come with the monitor and CPU as one unit, like a big box with a window. These are often more convenient and take up less space than your standard computer made up of several components. Also, a single unit means fewer cables to worry about connecting.

Another alternative to the larger computers is a **laptop** computer. This is an "all-in-one" unit as well, with a much smaller CPU, monitor, and keyboard, and it is usually very light, maybe no more than six to seven pounds. The best part about a laptop computer is that you can carry it around with you, in a special carrying case that is like a briefcase or bookbag, and you have the convenience of a computer wherever you go. The down side of a laptop, for some people, is the small size of everything. You have to get used to typing on a smaller keyboard and looking at things on a smaller screen.

Here are the main things you need to know, or have handy, about the personal computer and the basic features you should request if your goal is to get online:

	IBM Compatible Computer	Macintosh Computer
Hard drive size	500 megabytes* at least or even 1 gigabyte† or more	500 megabytes at least
Processor speed (CPU)	Pentium or Pentium Pro (486 are nearly obsolete)	at least 68020 Motorola CISC or Power PC
Operating System (OS)	Windows 95 is best (Windows 3.1 is okay)	at least System 7.5
RAM‡	8 Megs minimum§ (16–32 recommended)	8 Megs min. (16–32 recommended)
For audio	Get audio card and speakers	built in
For video	Get video card (with at least 1 MB RAM)	built in
Monitor	at least 15″ (unless a laptop)	same as PC

*1 byte=8 bits; 1 kilobyte (KB)=1024 bytes; 1 megabyte (MB)=1024 KB or about 1 million bytes
†1 gigabyte (GB)=1024 MB or about 1 billion bytes
‡RAM is Random Access Memory. Think of RAM as desk space and your computer hard drive as file cabinet space. The more RAM you have, the more programs you can run at the same time. But to save more things you need a bigger hard drive.
§Megs or MB is short for megabytes (Gigs or GB is short for gigabytes).

If any of this is too confusing, don't worry. The salesperson will know what it all means. Just remember that you don't have to get the latest and greatest of anything in order to access the Internet. The table above, however, lists recommended requirements.

What's a Modem?

Besides the computer itself, the other important piece of hardware or peripheral you need in order to get online is a **modem**, which is the appliance that helps your computer connect to and communicate with other computers.

Picture This: Think about the telephone. You pick up an appliance with numbers on it and you hear a dial tone, you dial a number and you hear the phone ring, then someone picks up a phone on the other end. He or she can hear you speak and you can hear that person speak, but how?

Well, your phone changes your voice into tiny bits of digital data or information that is then sent quickly over the phone lines and out comes your voice on the other end. The process is reversed when someone is speaking to you.

If you've worked in an office or have a home office, you can also think of how a fax works: You feed a document into it, dial a number, and your fax machine talks to another fax machine. Then the document is fed through the first machine, the images on the paper are converted into bits of digital data, and the data are transported through the phone line from your fax machine to the other one. On the other end, the digital data are received, then translated back into a facsimile of the original document.

A modem operates on the same principle as a phone or a fax machine, but it takes the digital data from your computer, instead of your voice or paper, and translates the data so they can be sent over the phone or data lines to another computer and vice versa.

A modem can be external or internal. The external modem looks like a small box, usually a little larger than a deck of playing cards, that attaches to your computer with a cable into a **communications port**, which is just an outlet on the back or side of your computer's CPU where you can plug it in. With an external modem, you can see lights flashing, which usually lets you know when it's working.

An internal modem looks like a thin card and it must be inserted into the CPU of your computer. I never recommend taking apart your own computer unless you really know what you're doing. Get a professional to install your internal modem. This should only cost you between $25 and $50. These days, many computers are sold with internal modems already installed. Keep in mind that preinstalled internal modems might not be the newest or fastest model, but they usually work well with the computer you buy.

Eenie Meenie Miney Modem . . .

Two of the top modem companies are US Robotics and Global Village, but as long as you get a modem that is "Hayes compatible," which means it meets certain standards (this description is usually written on the packaging for the modem), you should be able to purchase a product that is compatible with your computer.

You also want to get a modem that operates at a reasonable speed, because when you are online, you are **downloading** and **uploading** data to and from your computer. Downloading means transferring data from another computer to your own, while uploading is the opposite, transferring data from your computer to another one. Some data files are larger than others, particularly graphics, audio, and video files; therefore, to fully appreciate all the features of going online, you need to have a "fast" modem.

Currently, the most common modem speed is a 36,600 Kbps (kilobits or thousand **bits** per second) modem (or 33.6 for short). A bit is the smallest unit used to measure computer data. Some people are still using 28.8 Kbps, 14.4 Kbps, or even 9600 bps modems, which definitely work but they also transfer data very slowly, depending on what you are trying to do online, and can really test your patience.

Modem shopping tip: For a 33.6 or 28.8 Kbps modem, make sure it operates on the v.34 protocol, which is the international standard (for 14.4 Kbps, v.32 is the standard).

You should base your purchasing decisions first and foremost on your budget, then do research on the quality products that fit into it. Besides computer stores, you can often find good deals on computers and peripherals through mail-order computer companies such as Gateway 2000 (1-800-846-2036) or through computer-supply catalogs such as MicroWarehouse for IBM compatibles (1-800-367-7080).

Remember, buying the latest and greatest modem or computer is not always the wisest decision—products on the "cutting edge" tend to be less reliable and need to have the "bugs" worked out and fixed.

Getting Hardware Advice

Asking friends and colleagues for recommendations about computers and modems is risky business. Everyone has his or her own personal opinions about hardware, and everyone feels that his or her preferences are the best and only options for the rest of us. Beware of fanatical hardware fans! And be even more wary of the person who recommends that you wait another month or two—or another year—before you buy a computer because of the "big, new changes" that will make anything you buy right now obsolete. I've met so many women who have been waiting years to buy a computer because of this "fear of obsolescence."

Bottom line: If you buy a computer that works now, chances are it will work well for several years. Maybe it won't slice and dice and make julienne fries like the newest model that comes out next month, but any computer being sold with the basic features already mentioned are functional and can definitely get you online.

Up until two years ago, my first computer worked perfectly

well for word processing and playing games at the ripe old age of over six years. Now, my oldest computer is my Macintosh Powerbook 180 (laptop), which is at least four years old, and although it has a black-and-white monitor, it still handles word processing and other programs as well as connecting to the Internet with a 9600 modem (slow, but it works).

The Mac vs. IBM-Compatible Argument

The debate between Macintosh lovers and users of IBM-compatible computers has been an ongoing feud for more than ten years. Which type of computer is better? IBM-compatible computers are the most common, mainly because IBM was one of the first major corporations to put out personal computers (or PCs). Today, we still say IBM-compatible computers but usually mean brand-name computers in addition to IBM, such as Compaq, Gateway 2000, Micron, or Dell.

A little background: IBM-compatible computers used to be text-only, meaning when you started up and used your computer, you saw only text and used text commands to get around and perform functions—no mouse! These computers used an **operating system** called DOS, for disk operating system. Boring!

When the Macintosh computer came out, it used a different operating system—one that was based on graphics, so instead of typing commands to make things happen, you could use a "mouse" to point and click on icons. Something to know about Macs: For a while, a company called Power Computing was carrying computers using the Macintosh operating system. But Apple recently decided they were going to put a stop to another company selling Mac "clones."

Eventually, Windows arrived, a new operating system that covered up the boring DOS, had a graphical interface like Macintosh computers, and used a mouse as well. Windows 95 is now becoming the most popular operating system. Which is better? You really have to decide for yourself.

Here's a very basic checklist to help you decide between an IBM-compatible PC and a Macintosh computer.

PC might be better if . . .	Mac might be better if . . .
1. You're business-oriented	1. You're creative and arts-oriented
2. You use more business applications like word processing and spreadsheets	2. You use more graphics, arts, and layout programs
3. You're doing accounting, tracking inventory, or using a database program	3. You're laying out a magazine or designing a brochure

In all fairness, PCs do work for creative applications and Macintosh computers do work for business applications. However, when you go into an office, you will find all the secretaries and the accounting department using the PC and the art department using the Macintosh.

Remember that the best way to decide is to try each one for yourself. Also, check the different programs and activities you'd like to do on your computer and see which computer accommodates those activities.

Where to Buy?

You have several options where you can buy a computer:

Where	Pro	Con
Computer store	Helpful salespeople; you can look at everything	Overzealous salespeople; hard to price shop
Catalog	Helpful salespeople; sometimes better deals	You can't see before buying
Secondhand from a business	Usually reliable computers; can be pretty recent models	Probably can't get warranties or instructions, unless they saved
Secondhand from a friend	Hopefully someone you can trust who will help set it up	Probably can't get warranties or instructions, unless they saved

Places to buy your computer and peripherals:

Stores

CompUSA
1-800-266-7872

Computer City
1-800-843-2489 (for store locations)

Computer Company/Catalog

Dell
1-800-879-3355
http://www.dell.com/ (See Chapter 6 for information about
   Web addresses)

Gateway 2000
1-800-846-2000
http://www.gateway2000.com/

IBM Consumer Division
1-800-426-7235
http://www.pc.ibm.com/

Internet Shopping Network
http://www.isn.com/ (online only)

MacWarehouse catalog
1-800-255-6227 (for Macs)
http://www.warehouse.com/macwarehouse/

MicroWarehouse catalog
1-800-367-7080 (for IBM compatibles)
http://www.warehouse.com/microwarehouse/

Micron
1-800-438-3343
http://www.micron.com/

Compaq (more for your business computer)
1-800-888-0396
http://www.compaq.com/

Item #2: Software

So if the hardware is the tangible stuff of your computer—the
walls, doors, windows, and electrical wiring of your house—

then the software is the intangible stuff inside the computer that performs specific functions.

Picture This: In your house, think of your appliances and their functions—for example, the refrigerator keeps food cold, the electric can opener opens cans, the blender, the oven, even the television and telephone. The difference between the appliances in your home and the software in your computer is simply that you can see and hold your appliances but you cannot see or hold software **applications**. Still, the idea that they perform a particular function is the same.

A common software application is a word processing program like Microsoft Word or WordPerfect. The main software you need to get online is **communications software**.

Most computers come with basic communications or "comm" software already installed, or when you install your modem, some comm software is often included. Some brand names of communications software programs are, for the Macintosh: Microphone and ZTerm; for Windows: Terminal, ProComm Plus, and WinnComm.

Basic comm software needs to be **configured**, which means you need to set the preferences telling it what number to dial and what settings to use when you are transferring information. Just like you have to program a VCR to tape what you want, you have to set the communications software to dial and connect to another computer a certain way.

The **settings** you need to use with your communications software are usually provided by your online service provider; in some cases, it is done automatically by an online service's special software when you install it on your computer and connect to the online system for the first time.

Item #3: Phone line

If you are going online at home, chances are you will be using a normal phone line to dial into your provider. You don't need a special type of phone line to simply dial up an online service, but you may want to get an additional phone line to handle your online activity. Some people use only one phone line at home for phone calls, faxes, and online access, but that means juggling your time online.

If you are going online pretty infrequently, then you don't need a second line. You can get a two-socket phone jack so you can keep both your phone and modem plugged in at the same time. This way, you won't forget to plug the phone back in because you don't have to unplug it to use your modem.

When you are online, anyone calling into that line will get a busy signal if you don't have call waiting. If you do have call waiting, it's best to disable it or your connection online will be broken in the middle of something important. Check with your local phone company on simple ways to temporarily disable your call-waiting system if you don't want to be interrupted while you are online.

What's the Buzz?

When your computer, via your modem, dials up to connect online, you often hear a screeching and buzzing sound after the initial dial tone. In techie terms, this noise is signaling that your computer and another computer are trying to establish a "handshake." In simple terms, your computer is trying to make a connection.

When your computer connects to the Internet, first you are activating the communications software that talks to your modem, telling it to dial the phone number to your online service provider (the company you pay for the connection to the Internet). Then the modem turns the job back over to the communications software program to give the online service the right "log in" information, such as your userid or user identification or account name and your password.

Picture This: Back to the road analogy, your objective is to travel to another town. From your home, you get into your car, start it up, drive onto the road, use the proper signals, and follow the correct rules of the road to get to the on-ramp to the highway;

then you signal and merge into traffic on the highway. At this instance, the car is your communications software and the on-ramp is the first computer you access to get online, to get onto that highway. That leads us to . . .

Item #4: Account with an Online Provider

The missing piece of the whole puzzle of getting online is that you need an account with a company to get the online access you want. Why do you need to go through a company to get online?

Think of your online service provider as another type of phone or cable company. They offer you access to services, and you have several from which to choose. They probably offer special deals and frills or claim to offer better features than the competition to entice you to subscribe to their service. They bill you monthly for their service. And just like a phone company, online service providers are competing for your money.

There are two main kinds of online service providers: (1) commercial online services, or COSs (a destination along the highway), and (2) Internet service providers, ISPs (the on-ramp to get onto the highway). After I define the two main kinds of online service providers, I'll mention a few that are not as common but which you may want to explore.

Wrapup

The four main things you need to get online are:

1. Computer and modem (hardware)
2. Software (programs that perform functions on your computer)
3. Phone line
4. Account with an online service provider

We've talked about the things you need to get online. Now let's find out more about online service providers so we can actually get there!

Chapter 3   Now Entering Cyberspace: Finding the Road There

Commercial Online Services

Picture This: A commercial online service (COS) is like a stop off the main highway where you might find hotels, restaurants, an information center with maps, maybe a playground for the kids or a video arcade, a magazine rack, and so on. From a COS, you can also get back on the highway, but you're actually supposed to "hang out," spend time and money, and use all the facilities there.

In the Introduction, I explained how I got online by subscribing to several services (I was trying them out), the largest being America Online. America Online (AOL) is a very popular commercial online service.

Initially, commercial online services were set up so you paid a monthly fee to subscribe, which meant that you were allowed access to their private computers and databases and they would bill you hourly on top of a monthly subscription fee. These days, commercial online service rates are changing, often to a flat monthly fee, in order to stay competitive and to win or keep your business, much like phone companies are continually trying to give you special deals.

Other large COSs similar to America Online include Prodigy, CompuServe, and the Microsoft Network.

What's on a Commercial Online Service?

Because COSs see themselves as "destinations," they try to be more visually appealing, more fun and exciting, and more useful than their competitors. They contain forums or areas of interest based around a particular topic, like cooking or health, to entice you to read. Then they create ways for you to talk to other people about the topics, such as on posting boards where you can leave messages about the best recipes on a budget or new developments in medical research.

To enhance your online experience within COSs, they also have live chatrooms so you can actually meet and "talk" to people online in "real time" just by typing what you want to say; you can even go to scheduled special live chats with experts or celebrity guests on specific topics. These live chats are actually happening as you read and type.

Each COS is also like a TV network, in that it is trying to appeal to a specific audience. Although each service tries to be everything to everyone, they are different from one another.

Here's a very quick overview of the top four commercial online services: America Online, Prodigy, CompuServe, and the Microsoft Network. This is by no means an extensive resource list. The best way to find out about the features on any service is to try them out for a few weeks. Note that most of the major services offer some free hours for the first month that you subscribe to their service.

COS:	America Online
Type of Audience:	Broad, mass appeal
Resources:	Dictionaries, encyclopedias, a Yellow Pages directory, kids, health, shopping, travel, and a new women's area called Electra.
Entertainment:	ABC-TV, New York Times Online, *Car & Driver*, *Woman's Day*, MTV, *Late Night with David Letterman*, and Rosie O'Donnell. Celebrities and big, brand names draw a young, active crowd.
Community:	Chat makes up 60 percent of AOL usage and is easy to use, with Instant Messaging so you can instantly send a personal message to any other member who is on the service at the same time.

COS:	Prodigy
Type of Audience:	Was very family-oriented but opened up to the Internet so not as focused anymore
Resources:	Business & Finance, Kids, Travel, Entertainment, Technology
Entertainment:	Well-organized links to websites
Community:	The Prodigy chat is based on IRC (Internet relay chat) with over 150 approved rooms as well as access to rooms available on the Net.
COS:	CompuServe
Type of Audience:	Business and professional, librarians and researchers
Resources:	Best overseas access; good financial, medical, and legal databases, but usually at an additional charge
Entertainment:	Computer magazines, general interest publications, travel—fun and entertainment is not really at the heart of this service
Community:	Lively discussions on everything from computers to home-based business to design.
COS:	Microsoft Network
Type of Audience:	Trying for mass appeal
Resources:	Not very extensive reference databases with the exception of Microsoft's *Encarta* encyclopedia, parenting handbook, wine guide
Entertainment:	Movies, music
Community:	An easy format like AOL with bulletin boards, chatrooms, even international chats.

My First Day on AOL

When I first went onto America Online (AOL), I was truly overwhelmed but very excited. I felt as if I had entered a big city, and I didn't know where to go or where the buttons would lead me, even though they were clearly marked and easy to navigate.

I ended up in a chatroom and watched in amazement as names of users began to flash across the screen and then their conversations began to appear. In this main chatroom or "lobby," the conversation wasn't really much different from an open social setting where no one really knows anyone else.

Not knowing the proper protocol for online behavior or "netiquette" (see Chapter 9), I was really afraid to do anything for fear I'd do the wrong thing. Finally, I decided to say hello and typed the message, pressed the send button, and watched my screen name appear (NYCwriter) followed by my incredibly original first message:

`"Hi."`

Immediately, responses began to appear on my computer screen, mixed up in between messages from other people in other conversations (the art of chat is explained in Chapter 7). The responses to me included:

`"You're in NYC? Where?"`
`"I used to live in NYC."`
`"What do you write?"`

I was chatting online! What was interesting about my first live online chat was that it led me to meet one of my online "mentors." When I responded that I was working on a book about domestic violence, someone in the chatroom said, "You should really talk to EvaS—email her."

I emailed EvaS (sent electronic mail, see Chapter 4), and it turned out that EvaS was Eva Shaderowfsky, a woman who hosted weekly women's online conferences in a chatroom on America Online. She hosted special guests in her chats on a variety of topics where the "audience" in the chatroom could ask questions and have a formal discussion. I had made my first friend in "cyberspace" and discovered a new activity online (more about Eva in Chapter 13).

Connecting to a COS

Commercial online services usually give you their special **proprietary** or "private" software for free because they make their money when you subscribe to their service, not from buying the software. Their special software is a frills version of the regular communications software mentioned earlier. With their special software, you end up getting more bells and whistles.

For example, the software from a COS usually gives you an attractive (that's a matter of opinion, of course) "graphical interface" to their service, which means instead of seeing only text on your computer screen, you also see graphics, such as buttons you can click on and icons that represent the different parts of their service.

When you install the special communications software from a COS, you are taken through an automatic, easy, step-by-step subscription process that includes checking your modem and configuring your settings. On America Online, for example, the software tells your modem to dial right into an 800 number to help you determine the local dial-up access phone number into AOL that is closest to where you live.

Then you are asked by the software program to give your name, address, and credit card number (see "Online Safety Tips" in Chapter 8) and to choose the payment plan you'd like to use.

You need Windows on an IBM-compatible computer or a Macintosh computer to access a COS with all of the graphics, but some of the services still allow you to log in using DOS systems with text-based commands.

You can call the services directly using their toll-free number in the United States to find out what services they offer that best suit your needs and your computer setup. Some COSs let you try their service for free the first month, which is yet another way they entice you to become a member of their service. If you have the time, you may want to sign on with a couple of the main online services and try each of them out, then cancel the accounts of the services you don't like.

Be careful, however, to make sure that they cancel your subscription and that their monthly charges for the services you cancel do not continue to appear on your credit card bill.

Toll-free numbers in the United States for the four most popular commercial online services and their prices are:

Service	Number	Basic Pricing (subject to change)
America Online	800-827-6364	$19.95 unlimited usage
		$9.95 for first 5 hrs.,
		$2.95 for each add'l hr.
		$4.95 for first 3 hrs.,
		$2.50 for each add'l hr.
CompuServe	800-848-8990	$24.95 for first 20 hrs.,
		$1.95 for each add'l hr.
		$9.95 for first 5 hrs.,
		$2.95 for each add'l hr.
Microsoft Network	800-386-5550	$19.95 unlimited usage
		$6.95 for first 5 hrs.,
		$2.50 for each add'l hr.
Prodigy Classic (the COS)	800-776-3449	$19.95 unlimited usage
		$9.95 for first 5 hrs.,
		$2.95 for each add'l hr.
Prodigy Internet (the ISP)	800-776-3449	$19.95 unlimited usage
		$9.95 for first 10 hrs.,
		$2.50 for each add'l hr.

Check with each service for up-to-date pricing.

Paying for a COS

Most commercial online services offer local dial-up numbers, which mean that when you connect to them, you are technically making a local phone call to a service that reroutes your connection directly to the COS's computers, usually in another state. This means that your only online charges should be the monthly fees set forth by the particular service and not long-distance phone calls. In some rural areas, however, this number is still a long-distance toll call.

Pricing for the commercial online services has changed dramatically in the last several years. As mentioned before, most services used to charge you an hourly rate on top of a monthly fee for subscribing to their service. Even though they would entice you with some free hours each month (five free hours was most common), that time would quickly run out as you did more and more things online. Suddenly you were being charged for every hour online (although it was usually still cheaper than making a long-distance call). People's online service bills began running between $30 and $150 a month, depending on their usage.

Now, in order to stay competitive and keep you as a customer, commercial online services are changing to a flat monthly rate with only additional charges for some "premium" features, special areas or services they feel are worth the extra money and are betting that you will as well—such as a news clipping service for busy executives. Although rates change often, chances are online service monthly fees should not exceed a basic cable television charge, and you'll find those charges on your credit card bills, not your phone bills.

Long Distance vs. Local Access

Some areas in the United States do not have local access numbers to the top commercial online services, particularly remote areas. COSs are constantly trying to expand their services into rural areas as well as into other countries to give cheap, affordable online access to more people. In rural areas and countries outside of the United States, the lack of stable and modern phone systems often makes getting access online a little more difficult.

If you are accessing a commercial online service from a remote area and have to use a long-distance access number, you may have to be more disciplined in the way you go online. Use a timer by your computer to set online time limits for yourself, make a list of your goals for going online before logging on, and try to do some of your work "offline," such as saving documents you find online onto your hard drive and reading them or printing them once you have logged off (see Chapter 4 for tips on composing and reading your email offline).

Sometimes, if you are in a remote area, commercial online services might not be the best solution for you.

The second most common way of getting online is through an Internet service provider.

Internet Service Providers

Internet service providers, or ISPs, come in many shapes and sizes offering many different prices and services. While a COS is like a stop off the highway, an ISP is like the ramp to get onto the highway: nothing to really look at or do, rather a way to get to the Internet.

You can often find an ISP in your immediate vicinity since more and more are popping up in cities around the world every week, it seems. ISPs are basically companies that usually don't offer frills, bells, and whistles but instead offer direct access to the Internet.

Picture This: An ISP is a "gateway" or an "on-ramp." When you connect with a COS, you are going into its computer system and often "staying there," accessing the vast amounts of varied information that it has gathered and created for you. When you connect to an ISP, you are usually making a quick connection to their Internet access service and then sent out directly to the nebulous space of the Internet.

Often, people prefer to start with a COS because they feel they are entering a defined and well-organized space. Then they "graduate" to an ISP to venture directly to the Internet, which is far from defined or organized. Some people remain on a COS because it's so easy to use, while others have both a COS account to serve certain needs like participating in a weekly support group online and an ISP connection to perform other functions like doing quick international research.

If the idea of an ISP seems too forbidding for you right now, you can skip the rest of this chapter until you're more familiar with your COS.

As the Internet is made more popular because of the World Wide Web (see Chapter 6), commercial online services need to find more ways to make their services seem interesting. ISPs are getting more business because they are the most direct way to the Internet and the Web. Most ISPs are local; however, there are a few with a national or nearly national reach.

Some National Internet Service Providers

These service providers have local access numbers across the country so they are considered "national." This means you can dial into their service from different numbers or an 800 number from other cities in the United States.

BBN Planet Corporation	AT&T World Net
800-472-2565	800-967-5363
http://www.bbnplanet.com/	http://www.att.com/worldnet
Earthlink Network	IBM.NET
800-395-8425	800-426-4968
http://www.earthlink.net/	http://www.ibm.net/
Mindspring	MCI One
800-719-4332	800-950-5555
http://www.mindspring.net	http://www.mcione.com

The easiest way to find a "local" ISP is to check with your local computer or software store—the staff usually knows the best ones and how to contact them. You can also check the advertisements in local newspapers, especially the free papers, to find special offers. Some local ISPs include Interport and Panix in New York City, TIAC in Boston, Best and Sirius in San Francisco, LibertyNet in Philadelphia, cyberTours in Maine, EnterAct in Chicago, SuperNet in Denver, HubNet in Texas, Westmoreland Online in Pittsburgh, and Florida Internet in Orlando and Miami. (You can find lists of ISPs at The List website at http://www.thelist.com and at http://www.cnet.com/Content/Reviews/Compare/ISP/, which is CNET's website where it has reviews of the best local ISP's.)

Tips: Your Hardware and Software Shopping List

Decide on a budget and stick with it, but don't base your budget on the cheapest computer. Buy the latest model that you can comfortably afford. Don't let the salesperson convince you that you have to get the latest, greatest computer or that the model you are getting will be obsolete in a few months. A computer by a reputable company is your best bet. And remember:

- For PC, get a Pentium or Pentium Pro chip; for Mac, a System 7.5 or higher.
- Modem should be at least 33.6 Kbps (28.8 is still acceptable), either internal or external and operating on the v.34 protocol (international standard).
- RAM should be at least 8 megs but preferably 16–32 megs.
- Hard drive size should be at least 500 megabytes and these days a gigabyte (1.5 million megabytes) of hard drive space is becoming more and more common.
- Get fax software to send faxes straight from your computer. Some fax software comes with OCR (optical character recognition) so you can edit faxes you receive in your computer.
- Get communications software (often comes with fax software).
- Get antivirus software—a must!
- Get a backup drive. Check out Zip drives or Jazz drives, which are inexpensive, large-capacity disk drives with special floppy disks that you can use for data storage or to backup your computer.

Tips: Your Internet Service Provider Checklist

- Local access number: Most large commercial online services have local numbers you can dial into; however, some rural areas do not have local access to national services. If that is the case, check into a local Internet service provider (ISP) instead. You don't want long-distance phone bills—trust me!
- If you are considering a local ISP, ask friends and business associates or your local computer store owner about its service.
- Ask the provider how long it has been in business and how many customers it has. You can also ask if you can test out the service for a few weeks for free. Many local services will work with you to get your business.
- Don't fall for the hypester providers with the loud commercials and too-good-to-be-true offers. Paying a few dollars a month more can be the difference between reliable connections with good customer service and a nightmare.
- First impressions count. Trust your gut instinct. If you are made to feel uncomfortable or rushed on the telephone with the customer service department, go elsewhere. You deserve customer service that is patient and clear.
- Make sure the provider allows connections at 28.8 Kbps or higher and SLIP or PPP connections (PPP is newer and considered more stable).

Getting Online for Free or Cheap

One of the big reasons people cite for not getting online is the cost. There are several things you can try to get cheaper or free online access.

Educational Perks

If you are a student at a college or university, chances are you are getting your online access for "free" or included in your tuition or at a very low cost. Educational institutions were among the first nongovernment or military groups to connect to the Internet, and these days they are offering the feature of being "wired" as yet another perk to attract more students.

Some modes of access through educational institutions are still text-based as opposed to graphical, but either way, there should be students or staff on campus who can guide you to getting connected and getting around.

Some universities and colleges have their own internal network system, in addition to outside access, where you can access information such as your grades, schedules of classes and events, a map of the campus, transcripts to lectures, and even classes taught online. More often than not, though, access through an educational institution is somewhat "censored"—that is, outside access can be monitored or limited for legal reasons.

In most cases, you have to be either a student or an alumnus to have Internet access on campus, but it's worth calling your local college or university to see what its guidelines are and if you qualify.

Local Bulletin Board Systems (BBS)

Bulletin board systems have been around for years and today look like very primitive commercial online services. They are usually text-only, often a little cryptic to navigate, and locally based. Many BBSs are literally run out of a person's home or garage—an individual who does it as a hobby or a side business since it is so easy to set up a BBS with a phone line, special software, and a regular computer.

BBSs can be free or have a very small access fee. They don't have local access numbers in other cities, so if the BBS is not in your city, chances are you will have to make a long-distance call to access it. You can find local BBSs at your local computer or software store or in a national print magazine called *Boardwatch* or the back of other Internet-oriented magazines.

The Freenet

On the local or regional front, Freenets are online services that are provided to the community at no cost (often subsidized by local government or local companies). Freenets have limited access to the Internet and can be set up like local BBSs—bulletin board systems that are text-based and a little awkward to get around.

On a Freenet, you can often connect to your community by accessing information for the school system, local government documents, schedules of events, or background on local businesses. Sometimes, just having email through a Freenet makes the service worthwhile even though its Internet access isn't much.

Libraries

In addition to wiring school systems, communities are also wiring public libraries for online access. While the access is free at libraries, it is usually text-only. It's also hard to get a chance at the computers, since this service is in so much demand.

People getting online through public libraries include senior citizens, students, people on a budget, and just about anyone who is curious and either can't afford a computer of their own or haven't yet bought one. At the Seattle public library, even the homeless are allowed to use the computer terminals to go online.

Cybercafes and Computer Centers

Some businesses, not necessarily computer businesses, are setting up terminals to offer online access. Cybercafes are places where you can get a bite to eat or a drink along with access to a computer terminal at your table. At a cybercafe, you can go online for an hourly fee ($5–$10 per hour), or some have special coin-operated terminals that give you five minutes for twenty-five cents.

Copy centers such as Kinko's are also beginning to offer Internet access for a fee through some of the computers they have set up for the public to use. There are also computer learning centers in some places where you can receive hands-on computer instruction and online access.

Eventually, as you use their services more and more, these cafes and centers become an expensive way of getting online, but they work well as an occasional or temporary solution to getting connected to the Internet to communicate or do research.

Sharing the Cost

If getting your own computer or getting an online account seems far too expensive, maybe you know a friend or family member with whom you can share the expense. Buying a computer together needs some coordinating and agreeing on things, such as what type of computer to get, where you will keep the computer, and who has access to it and when.

Sharing a commercial online service can be relatively easy because most COSs allow you to have several account names under one master account. That means you can have one name and your friend or family member can have another name; then, at the end of the month, you can split the bill. Sharing an account also means coordinating when you will each be online, but paying half the monthly fee is a big savings and well worth a little juggling.

If your area doesn't yet have a public computer that can be used for free or for a fee, then think about starting your own computer and coffee group. If you have a computer, open your home to your friends for an occasional lesson or practice run. You can all split the cost of the computer, of the instructor, and of the online access. Get creative and help one another get online!

Protecting Your Computer

A word of advice: Before you begin installing any software programs onto your computer and before you go online, install virus protection software. Although you may have heard that you can get a **computer virus** from the Internet, the reality is that you are more likely to get a virus on your computer through store-bought, packaged software or by sharing floppy disks with another computer than you are from going online.

A computer virus is a type of computer program that can wreak havoc on your computer's hard drive. If your computer is like your house and your hard drive is like the room in your house, imagine what the inside of your house might look like after an earthquake or, worse, a tornado. That's the kind of damage a computer virus can do to your hard drive. With a virus protection program like Disinfectant, SAM, or one provided by Norton Utilities (a software company), you can protect your computer from most of these nasty programs.

Keep in mind that computer viruses are created by people with time on their hands and are rarely an "accident." So if you ever receive or see a file on your computer that you cannot identify, it is best not to open it and just put it in the trash to delete it right away. Better to be safe than sorry.

Protecting Your Body

Carpal tunnel syndrome is one of the hazards of typing at a keyboard or engaging in any repetitive motion, which is why it is also called repetitive stress injury (RSI).

If you experience any of the following symptoms while typing at your keyboard, see a doctor immediately. You might be able to solve your problem with simple exercises, wrist braces, and more **ergonomic**, or "sound for the body," equipment. Or you may need surgery to repair damage in your wrists.

Some Symptoms of RSI
Pain in your arms, wrists, or hands
Pins and needles sensations, particular in your hands or fingers
Numbness in your arms, hands, or fingers
Stiffness in your wrists

Health Tips: Some Preventative Measures
In addition to RSI, being in front of the computer for long, uninterrupted periods of time can also cause headaches; muscle strain, particularly in your neck, shoulders, and back; and eyestrain. Here are some quick tips to help ward off physical

ailments from overusing the computer. Remember that these are not cures.

- Keep your typing at an easy pace, definitely not too fast. Then take periodic breaks from typing and stretch your arms, hands, and fingers—shaking them out and getting blood circulating. Exercise your eyes while you're at it, looking up, down, around, and away from the computer screen.
- Use a timer if you have to in order to remember to stand up and stretch at intervals. Raise your arms over your head and stretch your back muscles. Lean over and hang so your fingertips reach toward your toes and your head hangs gently from your neck. Then roll up very slowly. Take a couple of slow, deep breaths. Once every hour is a good time to stop and stretch.
- Check your posture. Sit up straight with some kind of cushion at your lower back to support it. Have both feet flat on the floor. Note the position of your monitor and make sure that you do not have to slouch in order to look at it.
- Check how you are reaching for your keyboard. You want the keyboard to be lower than your natural reach forward, with your fingertips resting lightly on the keyboard and your wrists relaxed.
- Get wrist guards or a wrist pad so you aren't resting your wrists on the edge of your keyboard or desk or so you avoid crooking your wrists up to type. You can also get special support for your computer's mouse.

Wrapup

The two most common ways to get online are:

> Commercial online service—America Online, Prodigy, Compu-Serve, MSN—a company that allows you to access its computer systems and also access the Internet

Internet service provider—local company giving direct access
to the Internet

Other ways to get online are:

Educational institution
Freenets, BBSs
Public library, schools
Cybercafes
Friends

So now we're online . . . what happens next?

part two

THINGS YOU CAN DO ONLINE

Accessing information is only one of the things you can do online, and it can be done in a variety of different and fun ways. Think of how you can go to the library and the different ways you can find the information you want: You can use the card catalog, you can ask the librarian, you can look through microfiche, or you can browse the bookshelves until something catches your eye.

The way you might look for things in a library is often based more on your personality and personal preference or how much time you have—there are no right or wrong ways to search, just faster or slower ones. But although accessing information is a great part of going online, communicating is the number one reason people cite for using the Internet, and email is their favorite thing to do online.

Chapter 4   The Ease of Email

What Is Email?

Email is short for electronic mail and it is the most popular tool on the Internet. Think of email as almost instant communication—a unique cross between a telephone call and a letter—that can be sent and received any time of the day or night and accessed whenever you want to go online.

Email is like a phone call because it is a transfer of bits of digital data through the phone lines, but it is more like sending a letter because it is actually an electronic document that you type, like in a word-processing program or on a typewriter. Instead of having to print out the letter, put it in an envelope, and mail it, you go online and transfer the data immediately.

Transferring data from your computer to another computer is known as **uploading**. The opposite, which is getting or receiving data onto your computer, is **downloading**.

Although email isn't always as immediate as a phone call, it is certainly faster than the regular postal mail, even faster than Federal Express. An email can arrive at its destination within a few minutes, although sometimes delays of up to an hour or so are possible. Many times email is delayed by the "gateway" or opening into or out of a particular server on the Internet.

Often, corporations and servers on private networks that have only a small connection to the Internet experience email delays. Also, since the Internet is such a loose network, the path your email takes to get to its destination can be varied and convoluted—though ultimately it does arrive rather quickly whether you are emailing from Nebraska to London or from California to the North Pole.

In addition to being fast, email is a very affordable way to communicate with anyone anywhere in the world, usually for the cost of a local phone call. Remember, however, that in order to send email, you must be connected to the Internet, and to be connected to the Internet, you must have all the right equipment, a phone line, and a monthly account with a company that will give you Internet or online access (detailed in Chapter 3).

Why Email?

With email, you can stay in touch with friends and relatives no matter where they are in the world, as long as they also have access to email. When my sister moved to Santa Fe from New York City, we emailed one another to stay in touch. We also attached files to our emails to continue working together on graphic design projects. I would design something, send her an email with a graphics file attached, and she would make corrections and improvements, then email the file back to me so I could use it.

My dad has email on his home computer and he sends me messages from Florida, where he lives. My mom just learned how to email me from her office. I get email from a cousin in California and from another cousin who lives only ten blocks away from me but whom I don't see very often because of my schedule.

I stay in touch with a girlfriend who moved to North Carolina, and we even collaborate on business projects using email to exchange ideas. I can't count the number of friends I've made through email whom I have never met face-to-face.

In business, I email clients with updates and reports, and I get email from people who would like to hire me as a consultant. Even in writing this book, I asked women around the world to email me their stories about going online so I could include some of their personal stories (see Chapters 13–22). The possibilities of communicating through email are endless!

From: Sue Anderson, MIS Training Coordinator

I have 2 daughters in college. When I learned that they had email access, I wanted to email them. That is what drove me to get online in Dec 1995.

My daughters write more details about their lives and feelings in emails than they ever say over the phone. It is like the old-fashioned letter-writing days. You can keep rereading them, unlike a phone call that is over when you hang up. Plus, as a mother, I get to lecture to my heart's content and they cannot hang up on me!

So How Do You Email?

For every activity you perform online, you need the right tool. And the tools that help you do things online are software programs—just like when you try to do something on your computer, you need word-processing software to type a letter or accounting software to manage your money.

Email software comes in many shapes, sizes, and styles and can work on IBM-compatible computers running DOS (text based), PCs with Windows 3.1 or 95, or Macintosh computers. Some of the more common text-based email programs are ELM and PINE, which are used most often in educational institutions, government agencies, and nonprofit organizations.

Commercial online services usually have their own fancy email programs built right into the free software they give you, which has graphics and pictures so it's easy to install and use. The more popular "freestanding" email programs are also graphical, so you can use your mouse or keyboard commands to perform functions. One of the top email software programs is Eudora, which is compatible with both PCs and Macs. (You can find the Eudora software online at ftp://ftp.qualcomm.com/ [see Chapter 5 about FTP] and http://www.eudora.com/ [see Chapter 6 about the World Wide Web] or you can get it for free from your local Internet service provider. You can also buy a commercial version that has more features than the free version.)

To use a freestanding email program, you still need to have a connection through an online service provider such as your local ISP, because without the connection online, you have no way to send the email you write on your computer to anyone else on the Internet. Remember: You must have an online connection by having an account with an online provider to make any of the software work on the Internet. Just having the software doesn't mean you're online.

If cost is an issue, you can try a free email service. The most popular national free email-only service is Juno at 1-800-654-5866 or http://www.juno.com/. You can connect to its service for free, with its software, but you're shown advertisements, which is how Juno covers the cost of its service.

How Your Email Program Works

All email programs have the two most basic functions: Send and Get Mail (although depending on the program you have, they might be called something slightly different). Remember that when email is sent to you, it is not in your computer. When you have an account with an online provider, it will provide you with an email box, which is actually space on its server (its computer). Your email remains on its server until you go online and "download it" onto your computer by using your email program.

Your freestanding email program may require you to "configure" or specify the settings so it includes the address for your online provider (who will give this information to you), your userid, which is also called your account or screen name, and your password. On commercial online services, these settings are usually preset when you start up your account, or they are set automatically when you first install the software and subscribe to the service online.

Once your email is on your computer, you can open your mail to read it. Each piece of email is a text file with a **header**, **footer**, and **body** that contains the message. The header tells you who the email is to, who it is from, the subject of the email, the date, and usually the time it was sent.

The rest of the header and footer includes the names of all the servers the email bounced through on its way to its destination, sort of like the cancellation marks that the post office puts on letters or the stickers they put on packages that travel through different countries.

The body of the email contains the content of the message, which is as long or as short, as witty or as dull as the writer makes it.

Sending Email

To send mail, you must first open a new, blank piece of email; then you can fill in the email address of the recipient and the subject of the email. The date and your name and email address are usually automatically in the header based on your settings. You can make sure your return address in your settings is correct by emailing yourself. When you get the email, like any email you receive, you can reply to it. In most programs, this function is simply called Reply.

When you are testing out your return address and you've received the email from yourself, next Reply to that email. By replying, your email program will open a new, blank email that is already addressed to the sender of the previous email. You can then edit the subject if you'd like and type your response to the message.

By sending this test email, you'll soon know if your return email address is correct—either you'll get the reply back in your email box or you'll end up with a mail-error message. If you get a bounced or returned email, double-check your return address and make sure you correct how it appears in your setting.

What Is an Email Address?

Before we go on, I've broken down the parts of an email address so you can better understand what all those letters and symbols mean.

Here's an example of one of my email addresses:
NYCwriter@aol.com

Say this: "NYCwriter **at** aol **dot** com" (decimals in email addresses are spoken as the word *dot*).

Now let's break down the email address:

NYCwriter This is my screen name (also called userid or account name). This is a name that I chose when I initially subscribed to the online service that is hosting this email address for me.

@ This is the "at" sign, the telltale sign that you are looking at an email address. Your account is housed "at" a host server that is owned by your online service provider.

aol.com This is the name of my host server. In this case, "aol" stands for America Online and ".com" stands for "commercial entity," which is a quick way to identify companies as opposed to nonprofit organizations (.org), educational institutions (.edu), and so on.

The name of the host server is also called a domain name, and every domain name has a suffix or "zone" at the end that tells you something about the people who own or run the host server. The three-digit suffix is not the only ending on a domain name. International accounts might have their country represented in the suffix, such as ".jp" for Japan, ".nl" for the Netherlands, and ".ca" for Canada (see the "Domain Name Suffixes" on page 239). There will be more about domain names in the section on the World Wide Web in Chapter 6.

Tips: Getting the Email Address

How do you find someone's email address to send them email? The best way is to ask them! But there are also online resources to track people down (see the end of Chapter 12). Some things to remember about email addresses:

- If someone belongs to a commercial online service, chances are he or she can send email within the service without putting the domain name or the format for email addresses, though this might vary with the system. In America Online, for example, members can send email to one another with just their screen name, but if you send email to them from outside AOL, you have to add "@aol.com" to their screen name. On CompuServe, members have numbers for their user name, such as 1234,123, but when you email them, you have to put 1234.123@compuserve.com (using a period instead of a comma).

- Email addresses are usually not case sensitive; however, it is best to follow the email address exactly as it is told to you. When are caps important? Often, email through a private server for a company is more sensitive, so be precise.
- There are never spaces between letters in email addresses. Therefore, you might see a dot or an underscore or "_" between letters such as:

Aliza_Sherman@cgim.com
aliza.sherman@cgim.com

If you don't put a symbol between letters, spaces are automatically eliminated.

Replying to Email

When you reply to email, some programs will place the original message to which you are replying in the body of the new email, often with some kind of symbol preceding each line of the email, such as a greater-than sign (>) or colons (::) to designate the old message.

Some programs also put a line above the old message, such as "You said on 'date' at 'time':" which reminds the sender of what was written, who wrote it, and what time it was sent. Keeping at least some of the previous message in your email reply is considered good manners on the Internet.

At 10:45am EST on April 5, 1998, you said:

>>I was wondering if anyone knew how to
>>find the best resources for teen girls
>>on the Internet. I'm searching for
>>something for my daughter.

Keep in mind that some people send and receive a lot of email, and any hint at who said what is helpful. I get hundreds of emails a day and send hundreds as well, and sometimes I receive an email that simply reads "I agree. Please send it," or "That would be great. Thanks," and I'm suddenly in a quandary. Who is this person, what is he or she talking about, and what is it that I obviously said I'd do? I end up having to email back and say "I'm sorry, but I don't remember what this email was about." What else is a heavy-duty emailing grrl to do?

Other Email Features

In addition to sending, receiving, and replying to email, you can also forward email you have received, and some programs allow you to redirect the email. By forwarding, you are sending both the header, footer, and message to another person, like passing a note along.

You can trim some of the header and footer off the email and snip and edit the message as well, but it is proper to attribute the original email to the sender and to clearly show your edits by replacing a whole section with the word *snip* or *deleted*. By redirecting the email, you are allowing the recipient to reply directly to the sender of the original email instead of to you.

More sophisticated email programs also have great features, such as an address book (also called nicknames) where you can save the email addresses of the people you email most frequently, and even create "groups" where you can put many emails under one heading.

If you want to send the same email to your mom, dad, sister, brother, uncle, aunt, cousins, and grandma, you can compose your email, go to your address book, and choose a group you've made called My Family and send the email to everyone at once. You can also carbon copy and blind carbon copy people on emails, and both are fields in the header of the email.

Each email program has unique features, but the idea of how they work is virtually the same. Some email programs have additional features, such as email filtering where you can create separate directories or "boxes" for different types of email. If you receive a lot of email, you can create a box for "family," one for "clients," one for "potential clients," one for "friends," and so on. Think of these boxes as files within filing cabinets to better organize the emails you save.

Managing Lots of Email

Most people only have one email address; however, some people have several accounts and email addresses. An email program like Eudora allows you to jump between the different accounts you have on the Internet. Commercial online services usually let you create several names on a single account, which is different from having several email accounts. Some people have accounts with several commercial online services and Internet services. Why? The reasons vary from person to person.

For me, I have an AOL account because I help manage a forum on America Online for Avon's Breast Cancer Awareness Crusade and because I like to see what new features AOL offers. I also have accounts with CompuServe, MSN, and Prodigy to stay on top of what they're doing. Hey, it's my business to know what's going on so I can make recommendations to my clients. But I really only regularly check my personal email account. Still, I have one for personal and important email, one for general business, and another for people who visit my websites. Don't worry, I'm the exception to the rule. Most people have one account, two at most.

Wrapup

"Email" is what we call letters sent over phone lines from one computer to another. Features differ from one email program to the next, but if you have access to the Internet, you can send and retrieve, reply and forward email, as long as you have addressed it correctly.

Chapter 5   And Gopher, and FTP

In the Early Days of the Internet . . .

If email is the most popular online activity, then doing research and finding information is the second most popular thing to do. Where do people find information online? Well, if the Internet is a loose network of computers around the world that "serve up" information to the public, this information has to be organized in particular ways to be accessed.

Information on a server on the Internet is organized in a **database** or collections of data on a computer. The earliest databases were called Gopher and FTP databases.

Until the last few years, Internet databases were text-only, meaning that you searched through them by typing text commands. When you retrieved information from them, everything was in plain vanilla text. Gopher databases were one common way that information was organized in text on the Internet. When I first heard about Gopher, I thought that it stood for "Go For" as in "go for information." Actually, this type of database was first created at the University of Minnesota, and its school mascot is a gopher!

What's a Gopher?

Back in the old text-only days, you could search gopher sites by using the Gopher search tool where you could enter a keyword such as "woman" and get a list of gopher sites where that word appeared. Today, Gopher is not really being used by most people because it is considered outdated and more for heavy-duty research. Gopher is still popular in the academic world and on some smaller, closed network systems such as IGC (International Global Communications), a nonprofit service that has several topic-related databases, including Women's Net.

Examples of Gopher Site Addresses

```
Women's Net
gopher://gopher.igc.apc.org:70/11/women

Peace Net
gopher://gopher.igc.apc.org:70/11/peace

EcoNet
gopher://gopher.igc.apc.org:70/11/environment

ConflictNet
gopher://gopher.igc.apc.org:70/11/conflict

LaborNet
gopher://gopher.igc.apc.org:70/11/labor
```

To search and access gopher sites, you need to use special software tools, such as TurboGopher for Macs and HGopher for PCs. The website where you download TurboGopher is http://www.shadowmac.org/pub/mirrors/Info-Mac/_Internet/turbo-gopher-203.hqx; or go to http://www.winsite.com/info/pc/win3/winsock/hgoph24.zip to get HGopher. You can use your Web browser to access gopher sites (see Chapter 6). Be aware: The software might immediately start downloading onto your computer once you connect to these sites. You may have to search your computer's hard drive to find exactly where that software went, so make sure you jot down the name of the program.

FTP for You and Me

The other database that is more common on the Internet is the FTP database, which is perfect for downloading and uploading large files such as very large text files or software files. FTP stands for "file transfer protocol," which means it is the way to transfer files back and forth on the Internet. Today, FTP is used most often to download software, software upgrades, and other software tools that can be installed on your computer.

People frequent FTP sites to find everything from fonts, clip art, and other public domain graphics (available for public use) that are perfect for desktop publishing to computer games. **Anonymous FTP** is the term used for how you sign on to a computer on the Internet and copy public files from it. The Anonymous FTP service allows anyone in the world to log into specific parts of a server's hard drive "anonymously," which gives him or her limited access to files and archives of data.

Sharing computer programs and games or fonts on the Internet is common practice. Some people even create their own software, games, and fonts; they then offer them to the Internet community either for free or for a very small fee.

Software that is offered for free on the Internet is called **freeware**, and if the programmer requests a small fee in return for use, usually between $10 and $40, it is called **shareware**. There are public domain FTP databases that anyone can access, and you usually find them on the servers of colleges and universities, filled with all kinds of useful and fun programs. Major software companies such as Microsoft and Adobe have FTP databases where you can sometimes download upgrades to their software free or for a small fee.

Examples of FTP Site Addresses

```
ftp://mirrors.aol.com/pub/info-mac/
(AOL's FTP Mirror Site of Stanford Info Mac
Archive)

ftp://cica.indiana.edu
(the Center for Innovative Computer Applications
[CICA] at Indiana University in Bloomington)

ftp://ftp.qualcomm.com/
(Qualcomm, home of the popular email program
Eudora)
```

To search FTP sites, you can use Archie (yes, like Betty, Veronica, and Archie in the comics), which is an Internet software tool. To perform the FTP function—that is, to upload or download files using file transfer protocol—you need to use FTP software such as Fetch for Macs (http://www.shadowmac.org/pub/mirrors/Info-Mac/_Internet/fetch-302b2.hqx) and WinFTP for PCs (http://www.winsite.com/info/pc/win3/programr/winftp.zip/).

When you go to the sites to download the software, keep in mind that the software might immediately start downloading onto your computer as soon as you connect. Keep an eye on where you saved the software files you downloaded—make a note of the name of the files in case you have to do a search later. You can also use your Web browser to access FTP sites (see Chapter 6).

Keep in mind that Gopher and FTP are not only the names of types of databases on the Internet, they are also the names of the actions or tools you use to get to the information inside those databases.

You can say "I'm FTPing software from the Mac Archive that is an FTP database" or "I'm searching gopher sites with special Gopher software called TurboGopher." Both Gopher and FTP are useful in their own way, but neither of them can compare to the World Wide Web.

Wrapup

"Gopher" and "FTP" are types of databases used to organize and store text on the Internet. They are also the tools used to search those databases and transfer files to and from your computer.

Gopher sites are places where you can search for text documents on a variety of topics; however, they are becoming an obsolete means of transmitting electronic information other than for research because these days people generally want more than text with their information. You use Gopher software to search Gopher databases and to download or save information onto your computer from them.

FTP is useful as a tool for transferring large files to and from an FTP database. Usually, FTP databases contain software programs, games, fonts, and other large files that you can download onto your computer or upload into the FTP databases.

Techie Note: FTP is also the tool of choice used by people when building a website to transfer the pieces or files of the site to the host server.

We're starting to get a sense of the ways information is organized and accessed on the Internet. Now for the good stuff—the World Wide Web!

Chapter 6 The Wonders of the World Wide Web

So What Is the World Wide Web?

The World Wide Web (the Web, for short) is a multimedia, interactive version of the Internet. The databases of information that make up the Web are filled not only with text files or program files but also with graphics files and even audio and video files. Because Web databases are written in a special way—using something called HTML or hypertext markup language—when you retrieve data from a Web database or **website**, you end up with a multimedia presentation.

Multimedia refers to combining text, graphics, and other types of media so that instead of seeing plain vanilla text on your computer screen, you see all the chocolate chunks, nuts, whipped cream, and cherries (sorry, I couldn't resist)—a page with cool pictures and graphics that is designed and laid out similarly to a page created in desktop publishing. Even the simplest Web page is certainly more interesting than any text-only document.

What Are Links on Web Pages?

The feature that makes **navigating** or getting around the Web and websites so much easier than text databases are the links that connect pages together. The World Wide Web is actually much like a "web" because of these interlinked pages. Behind the scenes, links are lines of text on a page or images that are "programmed" through HTML to link to other pages. What you actually see on a Web page is text that is highlighted, in a different color, or underlined. This text is considered a "hot spot" or "hot link." You can find these by moving your cursor with your mouse; when it changes from an arrow to another symbol, such as a hand with a finger pointing, it signifies a "hot spot."

Picture This: Imagine you are reading a research paper or a book and you see a footnote at the bottom that references another paper or book. Now think of how convenient it would be if you could click on the footnote and—voilà!—you are immediately delivered the text of the next paper or the part of the book that is relevant to what you are reading.

Another way to think of links is to imagine you are watching television and you see a product that a character in the soap opera is using. What if you could click with your remote control and see information on that product? Or you are watching the news and you hear about a political figure and you want to know more about him than what is mentioned in the report. With a click of the remote control, you are then shown video about that person's life that gives you the background information you need.

The links on Web pages help create invisible links to other documents or files anywhere on the Web that are somehow related to the linked word. Those links can also open up sound files, video files, or animation in addition to text.

By moving your cursor across a page, you can find other hot spots that are not text links. Images such as graphics and photographs can be links as well. Sometimes you can see that an image is a link because it has a colored border around it. Usually the Web page has been programmed to hide the borders for "design" purposes. Without borders, the graphic should clue you in to the link by a button graphic that you can "press," or if you still don't see a link, you can move your cursor over the image or the page to see if the cursor changes, signifying a link.

Links are the primary way to move from one Web page to another. Links can bring you to pages within the same website or to pages located on other sites on other servers on other parts of the Internet. To follow a link, you simply click on it.

How do links work? Behind the scenes, the programming of the link tells your browser where to go next, either giving the destination of a page in the same database or giving the entire Web address to an entirely separate one. All you have to worry about, however, is pointing your cursor with your mouse and clicking your way to the next page.

Now you can begin to imagine the incredible scope of information available to you by simply pointing and clicking, pointing and clicking.

From: Kathryn Koromilas, teacher of English as a Second Language to adults in Australia

I began setting up my website—initially a site for my thoughts on gender and philosophy. I then set up a personal site and added some poetry. I also listed my favorite books on my site, one of which was "The Alchemist" by Paolo Coelho. He actually emailed me thanking me for the mention and also telling me I had misspelled his name. Then he invited me to link to his page from my page, which I did. That is the best thing about the Web, I think: making the world a little smaller. . . .

Viewing a Website

Websites consist of many, many files in databases, files inside of directories, files linking to other files, graphic files embedded into text files, and more, so you need software to sort through all of these separate files to make sense of them.

To access the information in a website, you first need to be connected online either through a commercial online service (COS) or through an Internet service provider (ISP). Once you are online, you then need a special software program to "view" the website contents.

The software used to view, **browse**, or **navigate** the Web is called a **Web browser**. Remember, a Web browser is your "window to the Web," but it can't connect you to the Internet. Your account with an online service provider connects you to the Internet, and then the Web browser helps you explore the Web and access the information you need.

The two most popular freestanding graphical Web browsers (meaning they are not part of the software for a COS and they allow you to see graphics) are **Netscape Navigator** and **Microsoft's Internet Explorer**. Which one is better? It's more a matter of personal preference than of one being better than the other in every way.

Where do you get a Web browser? You can download them for free off the World Wide Web or they can be provided to you on disk by your ISP or through an Internet kit that you can buy at your local software store. Remember, Web browsers are **free**, so if you decide to spend the money for an Internet kit, make sure it includes useful information and documentation that you couldn't otherwise get for free.

There is such a thing as a text-only browser (such as Lynx); however, we'll concentrate on graphical browsers so you can see all the features of the Web. You can still "shut off the graphics" if you want to browse the Web more quickly. Why does shutting off the graphics make Web browsing faster? Graphics and nontext files take longer to download onto your computer than plain text; you can "set your preferences" on your browser by choosing from the menu items at the top of your screen when your browser is open.

How Your Browser Works

When you are online and you open up a browser, you often find yourself at the website of the company that provided the browser or the company that manufactured the browser. This opening page of a website is called the **home page**, and companies set a browser to open to their home page as a smart marketing move.

For example, if you are using America Online to access the Web, as soon as you open, or **launch,** its Web browser, you see the home page or first page of the America Online website. When you use Netscape Navigator, you open onto the Netscape home page, and when you use Microsoft's Internet Explorer, you open onto Microsoft's home page. Usually, on those websites, you can find both information about the company and helpful guides and directories to things that are on the Web to help you find your way.

Once your browser is open, you should see a menu across the top of your screen followed by a row or two of buttons and an open field where you can type in a "location" or Web address. The rest of your computer screen is filled with the browser window, where you'll actually see the information from websites. The browser shows you all the elements that have been programmed into the database, and each page will include links, either text or graphic links, to help you navigate from page to page.

While each browser is slightly different, there are some basic features common to most browsers, although they may have different names. For example, looking at the top menu of words, you probably see some of the following commands:

File—If you select file, you have options such as:

New Web Browser—this opens up another window (you can have several browser windows open and be looking at several sites at one time)

Open Location—this is another way to put in a Web address and go to a website

Open File—this is how you can open up a file on your computer (perfect for when you are designing your own website)

Edit—Cut, copy, paste (helpful when you are copying information from a browser window)

View—Features such as:

Reload—If a Web page doesn't load properly, you can hit reload to try again.

Load Images—Sometimes images are too big; this enables you to shut off the option to load images automatically. You won't see the graphics, but you'll get to the information more quickly.

View Document Source—Believe it or not, you can see the "behind the scenes" language that makes each Web page a multimedia presentation. By viewing the source of a page, you see the HTML (hypertext markup language) and can learn how people program and design the pages of their website. Very helpful when you are learning to design your own site.

Go—Helpful feature that lets you navigate back to the last page you saw or advance to the next. Also, most browsers temporarily list the last several pages you just visited so you can jump back between those sites.

Bookmarks—Some browsers also call these cool links or favorite places. This feature allows you to save the addresses for websites you like so you can return to them anytime.

Options—Preferences can be set here, which means you can customize your browser, including the size of the font you see, what color text you'd like your browser to use, whether the top toolbars of buttons show up or not, if you want images to load automatically, and more.

Directory—Some browsers have their own bookmarks pre-installed to send you to special Web pages they've created to assist you with your Web exploration.

Window—Since you can open more than one browser window to view more than one site at a time, you can use this feature to choose between the different open windows of your browser.

Buttons on Your Browser

In addition to the pull-down menus, your browser also has convenient buttons on a toolbar at the top of the browser window which mirror some of the menu commands. These buttons include:

Back—Brings you to the previous page.

Forward—After you've gone back to a previous page, you can now go forward.

Home—Usually, the home button is set to take you to a default browser page, normally the company that created the browser; however, you can set your own home page in the Preferences.

Other than these common buttons, each browser may have different buttons based on its menu options.

Secrets of a Web Address (URL)

A Web address specifies the location of a Web database or website and is more commonly known as a **URL** or **uniform resource locator**, pronounced either "You-Are-El" or "Earl."

Picture This: An email address is like someone's P.O. Box number at the post office. A URL or Web address, on the other hand, is like the actual street or physical address or location for a site that can represent everything from a store, business, or library to an organization, educational institution, or individual home online.

A URL looks something like this:

```
http://www.cybergrrl.com/planet/index.html
```

Breakdown of a URL

http://—This means that the address you are looking at is for something written for hypertext transfer protocol, which is the "language of the Web."

www.—This is the name of the host computer or the server, also called the hostname.

cybergrrl—This is the second-level domain name that is

registered by an organization or entity with the InterNIC Registration Services. The domain name here is cybergrrl.com.

The domain name stands in the place of an **IP number** or address, which is the number assigned to servers on the Internet, like a zip code. Instead of having to remember a number, such as 133.24.44.9, it's easier to remember and use the domain name.

.com—This designates a top-level domain name, and describes the purpose of the organization or entity that owns the second-level name. A domain name may include other components between the hostname and the second-level domain name, which are called subdomains.

The suffix ".com" means that the server represents a commercial entity as opposed to ".edu," which is an educational institution, or ".org," which is a nonprofit organization.

/planet/—Remember that a website consists of many pages linked together. Some of these pages are inside other directories, just like the files on your own computer's hard drive. In this case, "planet" is a directory on the server at www.cybergrrl.com, and it can contain other files or directories.

index.html—This is the name of an actual file, a page within a website. The suffix ".html" (or ".htm" if the site was created on an IBM-compatible computer) tells your web browser "this is an HTML document, a page in a website." In this case, index.html is a file in the directory called planet.

Some URLs are very long. If you look at a URL closely, you will see that it contains all the elements described above, and that the length usually means that a particular page is inside a directory that is inside another directory inside yet another directory.

Remember, the telltale sign that an address represents a website is usually the "http://" in front.

Say this: "Aytch TeeTee Pee Colon Slash Slash"—not "backslash." Websites don't always have "www" in them, so don't rely on those letters to clue you in when you see a URL. For example, one of our websites is located at:

```
http://village.cybergrrl.com
```

Keep in mind that many people will leave off "http://" because all URLs start that way, and they just write or say the rest of the address: www.cybergrrl.com or village.cybergrrl.com

These days, you can access gopher and FTP sites using your Web browser. You can enter a Gopher address into your browser like this:

```
gopher://gopher.igc.apc.org:70/00/women/
Directory/directory
```

Or an FTP address as:

```
ftp://netscape.mcom.com
```

Both types of addresses can be read by your browser as if they were URLs or Web addresses.

You can use your Web browser to access both gopher and FTP sites. Often, you can link directly from a Web page into an FTP database, which is a common way for a site to give you a "front door" to access its larger files such as software and computer games.

What Does a Website Do?

Keep in mind that each website looks and operates differently, depending on how the site is programmed and how the pages are designed. The skills of the programmer or designer affect how attractive a page is, how easy it is to get around, how quickly the images load onto your computer, and how effective it is at doing what it is supposed to do.

What is a website supposed to do? Initially, HTML was created so that scientists and academics could link together their papers and reports so when they quoted from one another, they could make their footnotes link straight to the source. Linking information was the primary reason the Web was created.

Accessing the Web

Here is a quick rundown on how to access the Web:

1. First you need an account with an online service provider. Your provider can be a commercial online service (COS), which usually has a built-in Web browser or allows you to use a freestanding browser such as Microsoft's Internet Explorer or Netscape Navigator. Or your provider can be an Internet Service Provider (ISP) who furnishes you with free software including a freestanding browser.
2. Once you have set up your communications software (built into the software for COSs or given to you by ISPs), you need to dial into your provider's system and connect to its service so you are "online."
3. Once the connection is made (after all the screeching modem sounds), you may have to enter your userid/account name and password or they might already be saved when you set up or configure your communications software, so it might be automatic.
4. When you are accepted onto your provider's system, you can now "launch" or open your Web browser. Often, when you first open your Web browser, it is already set at a particular home page, usually the first page of the website of your provider or the creator of the Web browser (such as Microsoft or Netscape). You can change the home page setting through your browser's Options or Preferences to any page you like. I changed my home page from Netscape's page to Newspage, where I had a free account to access news headlines about the Internet, a fast way for me to access up-to-date information about my industry.

5. Many times, the home page of your provider or of your browser company has links to interesting or helpful sites to get you started exploring the Web.

Today, websites serve many purposes. Here are just a few types of websites you'll find online:

Educational (suffix: .edu)—Colleges, universities, high schools, middle schools, even elementary schools are putting up websites to show what they have to offer students. Find out about faculty, curriculums, scholarships, extracurricular activities, and often student-created sites. There are also educational resources that aren't connected to schools that are assembled by individuals or groups who gather information from many sources and put it all on one site.

For example, the Artemis Guide to Women's Studies Programs in the United States at http://www.interport.net/~kater/ was compiled by Kate Robinson, a graduate student who wanted to create a resource listing women's studies programs at colleges across the country. She built her website and included links to the websites of those colleges that offer a women's studies program. A company called Infonautics created a vast library resource called E-Library at http://www.elibrary.com, an educational website that is good for research but note that it charges a fee to use it.

Nonprofit (suffix: .org)—Organizations have discovered that a website is a good communications tool to let people around the world know about their mission, their work, and important issues. Most nonprofit websites include funding information and some even have a form to accept online donations.

Some sites, such as the website for NABCO (National Alliance of Breast Cancer Organizations) (http://www.nabco.org), offer useful services to visitors, such as an email breast health reminder. A woman who visits the NABCO site can fill out a form with her email address and the date and place of her last mammogram, including the phone number for the facility. In a year, the database behind the website will automatically email a reminder that it is time for her to have her yearly breast exam, including the place and phone number of the facility she last visited.

Personal (suffix varies, depends on Web server)—I have to say the greatest thing about the World Wide Web is that anybody can create his or her own website and put it online. A personal website is something different to each person who creates one.

When I first put up my personal website in January 1995, it contained several sections of information including:

- Domestic Violence Information—At the time, I was the executive director of a domestic violence awareness group and thought it was important to put a handbook, statistics, and a bibliography online for anybody who was affected by violence.
- My Favorite Things—Instead of talking about myself, I decided to post lists of things I liked with lots of links to related sites, such as Pre-Raphaelite art, Arthurian Legend, and London, England.
- Webgrrls—When I first went online, I tried to find websites by women to see what they put on their sites. When I found them, I created links to their sites from my website and called the group of women Webgrrls. A few months later, some of the women in the New York City area gathered at a local cybercafe to talk about our websites and the Internet, and an international organization was born. (See "Cybergrrl Resources on the Web" on page 217 for more details about Webgrrls.)

Other personal sites include tributes to favorite celebrities or sites devoted to a personal hobby, sport, or interest. Some people create resources on particular topics that are useful to a wide audience, such as Francine Gutliwick's *Yummyzine* website at http://www.yummyzine.com for busy working moms. It contains meal plans for each week, including recipes and shopping lists for the ingredients.

From: Lutgarde Gaddum-Mees

I am Lutgarde from Belgium, 49 years old. Married
for 29 years. I have two children, a son and a
daughter. When I was 14 years old I left school,
and started working at the factory. When I
married, I worked for two more years and then
stayed at home. Last year, I became interested in
the Internet. I received a lot of mail about it,
and so it began. My husband had a computer, and
he told me how it worked. I have made a few new
acquaintances via email. Now I am working on a new
website. There are a few links on it, also a link
to the Webgrrls. And a little story that our
little dog Kenzo tells for the children. I thought
it would be fun for the children, and they can
send an email to Kenzo. I am sure he will answer
them with an email. I am quite proud of myself
that I have achieved so much in such a short
period of time. So look at my website at
http://www.tornado.be/~gaddum/.

Business (suffix: .com)—Businesses are scrambling to try to find
a way to make money on the Internet and Web, but very few
have been successful . . . so far. People have mixed feelings about
businesses building websites, afraid that there will be too many
"ads" and "commercials" instead of meaningful sites.

The smartest businesses are taking the opportunity to build
useful communities and resources online in order to gain new,
loyal customers. By giving something back to the online community, a business can gain a lot of goodwill and positive media
exposure. When you go online, you can benefit from some of
these commercial sites, such as the Pampers site (http://www.pam-
pers.com) which contains useful parenting information.

Transaction sites—Some commercial sites offer products for
sale through the website with a secure server that allows you to

enter your credit card number on a form on the website. These days you can buy music CDs, books, flowers, gift items, clothes, even cars, all on the Web. You can even book an entire trip, including flight and hotel. I buy my movie tickets online through movie link (http://www.movielink.com).

Entertainment sites—Other commercial sites are built purely for entertainment, whether it is a site for playing online games, to give the latest movie gossip, or even offering online "soap operas." There are print magazines that have an online version as well as webzines, which are published exclusively on the Web. There are TV guides and movie directories, sites for writers, and online digital art galleries. There are sites about astrology, travel, fashion, and more, with new sites appearing on the Web every day.

Finding the Website You Want

With such a wealth of websites on a vast array of topics, how do you find what you're looking for? Luckily, some companies and individuals have set up websites that act as directories for other websites.

Yahoo (http://www.yahoo.com) is one of the more popular **searchable directories** that has thousands and thousands of links to other websites in its database, which you can search simply by typing in a search topic or word in a field on Yahoo's home page. The best thing about Yahoo is that it is categorized and alphabetized, so it's easy to search, but it isn't one of the largest directory sites.

Two of the larger directory sites are Lycos (http://www.lycos.com) and Alta Vista (http://www.altavista.digital.com). Both of these sites are more commonly known as **search engines** because they have special software programs that move through the Internet, automatically indexing all the Web pages they find out there. They aren't alphabetized or as carefully organized as Yahoo, but they can give you thousands of results. Other good search engines include Excite (http://www.excite.com) and InfoSeek (http://www.infoseek.com).

To learn how to "narrow" your search effectively, read the

instructions on each directory or search engine, usually behind a button called Options.

In 1995, when I was searching the Web for sites for women, I realized that most of the search sites were created by men, and their women's resources left much to be desired. So in September 1995, I created the first search site for women's websites and information online called Femina at http://www.femina.com. Today, the Femina site is managed by a "cybrarian," one of the new jobs created because of the Internet and the Web.

The Web consists of vast amounts of information that do not have a central directory, so individuals and companies try to create new ways of organizing the information to make it easier to search and find what you're looking for. Businesses and jobs are being created just to connect people to information.

Wrapup

Web databases, or sites, contain text, graphics, and even audio and video files. They are connected together by links, so that you can click on a word and be instantly transported to a different site.

Once you are online, you will need a Web browser to view the Web. This is a piece of software that acts as your "window to the Web." Then you can either type in a website's URL (address) in the browser or use a search engine to find the website you are looking for and to actually get to the site.

Chapter 7 Not Just Fun and Games in Forums and Chat

Besides connecting people to vast amounts of information—some great, some good, and some pretty useless—the Internet and the Web also connect people to other people.

When commercial online services started, in addition to email, members were actively communicating with other members in topic-related forums or **posting boards** (also known as bulletin boards and message boards) as well as in live, real-time **chatrooms**. Today, more and more websites are providing the same features as the commercial online services, including the posting boards and chat, although until recently they weren't as easy to use as those on the closed services with their special software and computer systems.

From: Christine Farrell, entrepreneur and consultant

I am going through a life change (divorce) and beginning again at the age of 50. I love the Internet and the possibilities, which I believe is only limited by our imagination. I know email has changed my way of thinking and the Internet will do the same. I am a little late getting wired, and have a ways to go, yet I think this is a much-needed skill for the future. I started with MSN, found bulletin boards that hosted similar interests such as an equine forum and quickly made friends. Here I found one of my best friends, who lives in Connecticut. I live in Washington State. We have never met, but correspond frequently.

Usenet, Web Boards, and the Art of Posting

Even before commercial online services appeared with posting boards, the Internet had its own version of these topic-related boards called **Usenet Newsgroups**, text-based boards. "Usenet" or "newsgroups," as they are called for short, are posting boards that are out on the Internet and not on closed, commercial online services (COSs), so they are international and accessible to anyone accessing the Internet. Despite the name, newsgroups are not necessarily places to discuss current events or news. Topics for newsgroups can range from skiing to cooking to camping to parenting.

(The following description of a posting board is a repeat from the book's Introduction, for those who didn't read it!)

Picture This: To visualize the concept of a posting board, imagine an actual bulletin board where people can tack messages each day and other people can stop by the board, read the messages, and tack on their own. Some of the messages might be questions for which people want answers, while others are stories or interesting information pertaining to the common topic. With an online posting board, the messages are electronic but the concept is the same.

When you first enter a posting board area, you see lines of text on your computer screen that usually include someone's name or nickname, the date and time, and the subject of the post, each line representing one post. You have to open the post (the process is slightly different with each service) before you can read it. You can usually tell what a post is about by the subject of the post.

Accessing the Newsgroups

Software called newsreaders is specifically made for reading newsgroups, but the great thing about your Web browser is that it is versatile enough to read most newsgroups on the Internet.

Commercial online services also have Internet areas where you can search newsgroups by topic and then access them through their own software.

Having the right software to read newsgroups is one thing, but being able to access or "receive" them is another. Often, your ability to access newsgroups is limited by your service provider. On COSs, for example, they may filter some of the "adult"-oriented newsgroups, while an Internet service provider (ISP) might carry only two thousand of the over ten thousand newsgroups that are currently available. You may have to contact your provider to gain access to a group you've read about but isn't showing up on your service.

The special software you need to read your newsgroups includes Newswatcher for Mac (http://www.shadowmac.org/pub/mirrors/Info-Mac/_Internet/newswatcher-216.hqx) and Trumpet NNTP Newsreader for the PC (http://www.winsite.com/info/pc/win3/util/wtpkt10a.zip/). If you have an account with a COS, however, the newsreader is built right into their software.

In addition to Internet-based text newsgroups, websites are offering Web-based threaded messaging boards. People stop by newsgroups or Web boards, read messages, then post a message of their own, either in response to an existing message or to ask a question or make a comment.

On any messaging board system, once people begin to respond to the same posts and a "conversation" begins to develop, the result is called a "thread." When you follow a thread, chances are you will see a fairly linear discussion, and you can usually identify threads by the "Subject" line such as:

```
Subject: Working Moms—Coping
Subject: RE: Working Moms—Coping
Subject: RE: (2) Working Moms—Coping
```

and so on. Good posting etiquette means making sure that the subject of your post is short and to the point so other people can easily guess the contents of the post. Another good manners tip is to change the subject if the conversation takes a different turn and your post contents shift from the original post. Sometimes, on a board, you might see a subject that looks like this:

```
Subject: Dealing with the Terrible Twos (Was:
Working Moms . . . )
```

Using good subjects is the best way to keep a conversation on track or to identify a new one when you are posting.

The Online Community

As you delve into Usenet or Web boards, you begin to understand how the messages flow and soon get a sense of entering a community. As people continuously post messages to a single board, they start to recognize one another, address each other by name (or nickname), begin to interact more, and soon set certain rules, spoken or unspoken, about how to behave on the board.

The phenomenon of a community forming out of a topic-specific posting board is truly one of the unique features of going online and is something to remember if you visit a board for the first time. It is best to "listen"—that is, read old posts first before you venture to post yourself.

Most boards have a link to an FAQ or frequently asked questions list, which is a document containing the most commonly asked questions about the board and its topic together with the answers.

Picture This: Think of entering a board as being similar to walking into a party or a meeting. Conversations have been going on and you need to be aware of the social rules and, by all means, be polite. Most boards have a strict rule against advertising, so I would not advise posting an ad for something you are trying to sell or you're bound to get flamed.

What Is Flaming?

Flaming is the unpleasant experience of receiving angry and annoying emails from people who have taken offense at the way you have posted in a public forum. Usually, you are less apt to get flamed simply for having a different opinion and more likely to be flamed for breaching proper Net etiquette or "netiquette." Later in this chapter we cover more about netiquette, and in Chapter 9 we talk about avoiding negative experiences online and, if they occur, how to deal with them.

The great thing about boards is that they are based around a single main topic, and chances are that if you participate, you will find other people with interests similar to your own. You can access the information on boards at your leisure because it is stored on someone else's computer for at least a few days if not weeks or more. If a board is very active, it might be cleared more often; however, the posts are usually archived somewhere for your review at any time.

Mailing Lists in Your Email Box

Another way to join topic-related conversations and communities is to subscribe to an **Internet mailing list**. The best way to describe a "mailing list" or "list," for short, is to imagine a "round-robin" email experience where everyone who subscribes to the list is automatically privy to all the emails sent to anyone on the list. The emails sent to the list actually arrive in your email box and can then be read as if you were reading a newsgroup or posting board.

When you read a list in your email box, you should pay attention to the subject lines and follow the threads, just like you do when reading newsgroups or posting boards.

Email lists differ from boards in that the messages or posts come directly to you, into your email box, which can be very convenient but also very overwhelming. Some lists are so active in conversation that you can receive in excess of a hundred emails a day, many of which may be more chatter than useful information. However, if you can manage the email, mailing lists are more immediate ways of communicating with other people on a particular topic.

Filtering the "Noise" of Mailing Lists

Your email software program might have a filtering feature, which comes in very handy when you subscribe to mailing lists. By using a filter in your email program, you can specify for emails from particular lists to be routed to another mailbox that you can create for each list you've joined.

Often, a list is filled with many unrelated posts or **noise**. To keep your participation in mailing lists meaningful, you should refrain from posting the "Me, too" responses. Even if you agree with someone who has posted to the list, there is no need to respond to everything when it is sent out to everyone. A private email to the poster saying "I agree" is okay now and then (as long as you keep some of the original post in the email message; otherwise you're guilty of unidentified email syndrome).

Moderated vs. Unmoderated Lists

Lists can be run in several ways. A list can be fully unmoderated, meaning someone has set the list up and rarely, if ever, steps in to manage the list. Chances are, however, the unmoderated list is actually just informally moderated. A list manager or moderator is the person who has set up the list or someone with the official position of moderator.

Moderating a list can be as informal as steering a conversation back onto the topic to stepping in to cool off a heated discussion to deleting bounced messages (when email addresses aren't working) to occasionally reminding members of the list's "rules" or how to unsubscribe to the list if they need to.

A moderated list is much more carefully maintained and the moderator's job is much more involved. A good moderator of a fully moderated list actually receives all messages first to review them before approving some of them to be sent to the entire list.

Being a full moderator is a big responsibility and can be very time-consuming, but fully moderated lists also usually contain the most relevant, on-topic, useful discussions of any lists.

Digests of Mailing Lists

If you are concerned about getting too many emails when you join a list, check to see if the list has a digest version. If it does, just subscribe to the list with the extra command as per the instructions to request the digest. The digest of a list sends you large emails containing multiple postings in the body of each email rather than getting five, ten, or twenty of them at once.

If you have already subscribed to the list and are overwhelmed by the email, contact the list moderator or owner, check the FAQ, or check the email you received when you first subscribed for information about a digest. Your last resort should be emailing the list to ask "Where's the digest?"

Joining Internet Mailing Lists

To be part of an Internet mailing list, you must subscribe. Internet mailing lists are run by using list software that is run on someone else's server or computer. He or she has installed the software onto the server and set it up to operate in a certain way; all you have to do is email a message to subscribe to the list and the software stores your email address.

When someone emails the list, that one email goes into the software and is broadcast to all of the subscribers. Then, when someone responds to a post and it is addressed to the list, that email goes into the software and is also broadcast to all subscribers.

Mailing lists have email addresses that you use when subscribing and different email addresses to use for posting messages. The way you subscribe and post differs depending on the software being used. The most common free software programs for lists are Majordomo, Listserv, and Smartlist. In order to subscribe to a list, you must first know the list name and the name of the server it is on—that is, the list subscription address.

For example, to subscribe to the Mom's List about parenting

and motherhood, you would: (1) send email to majordomo@ women.ca, and (2) put the following message in the body of your email:

```
subscribe mom-L
```

Note that for this particular list, you do not need to put your email address into the body of the email in the email message you have typed. From the steps above, we can assume that the software used to manage the Mom's List is Majordomo software. Other mailing list subscription directions might not clue you in to the type of software used. Note that this list requires approval from the list manager.

To subscribe to my list called Cyber Sisters (for women artists and writers), however, you must: (1) send email to cyber-sisters-request@cgim.com, and then (2) put the word SUBSCRIBE in the "Subject" of the email. I use the list software called smartlist.

Make sure you read the instructions carefully for each list before you subscribe, both about how to subscribe and how to unsubscribe.

Unsubscribing from a Mailing List

One of the most common mistakes online seems to be not knowing how to unsubscribe from an Internet mailing list once you have joined. The biggest mistake: posting your request to unsubscribe to the entire list. Ouch!

The best way to know how to properly unsubscribe from a list is to save the email you received the day you first subscribed to the list. That email contains all the instructions you need to post and unsubscribe, and often some tips and rules of the list.

If you have forgotten how to unsubscribe from a list or if you have been automatically subscribed to a list that you do not want to be on, email the list owner if you know the owner's direct email.

You can also try a few things to attempt to unsubscribe yourself. To unsubscribe, look at any email post you have received from the list and find the name of the list and the name of the server. Then try sending an email to:

```
majordomo@servername.com
```

Put the following in the email:

```
unsubscribe list-name
```

Chances are, if the list is a Majordomo list, you will be automatically unsubscribed. Or try this, send an email to:

```
list-name-request@servername.com
```

with UNSUBSCRIBE in the "Subject" or "Body" of the email (or both).

If you still cannot unsubscribe from the list, then it's okay to privately email the moderator—if you remember the email address. Or politely email one of the posters privately and ask for his or her help. The last resort is to email the list, but if you must, make sure you are polite about it. Remember that email goes out to hundreds of thousands of people, so you don't want to waste anyone's time.

The Great Chat Feature

Online, chat is carried out in chatrooms, where people gather and "talk" to each other by typing what they want to say. When they hit Return or Enter on their keyboard or click a button to Send or Speak, their words are posted in the room pretty much instantly for everyone in the chatroom to see.

Live online chat may have its limitations (sometimes slow, hindered by typing ability, unpredictable), but real-time chatting can prove a useful tool, a money-saver, and a fun pastime. You can find chat on commercial online services, such as America Online's People Connection. On AOL, when you first click on the People Connection button, you enter a "lobby," usually called something like "Lobby 641," which means it is the 641st lobby on the system, each lobby consisting of twenty-three people. AOL's service automatically builds a new lobby each time one fills up.

Lobbies or general chatrooms are considered to be a starting point and conversations there can be disjointed at best and non-sensical or inappropriate at worst. Most services also have pre-built, topic-related chatrooms where you can presumably go for more focused chats. The nature of the chatroom usually depends on how well it is monitored or moderated, how compelling the topic is, and how willing the "chatters" are to stay on topic.

A Current Events chatroom might have a great spontaneous discussion about a national event, with debate and discussion heating up in an intelligent, provocative way. But chances are, in an unmoderated or unsupervised chatroom, current events may quickly erode to the more typical talk about the weather, the "Where are you?" syndrome, and the too-common "sex/age" query where someone is asking for a count of males to females and ages to get a better sense of those to whom they would like to speak.

From: Charley Buntrock, graduate student

I'm constantly amazed at how much time and energy I spend on the Internet. I was especially busy last fall, when my boyfriend was in Australia, and in an attempt to save money, we used various chat services online on a daily basis. It was a lifesaver for our relationship, as well as our wallets. I've stayed away from the traditional chatrooms, although having a name like Charley has provided interesting fodder for my getting approached by women who think I'm a man when I'm playing online backgammon through chat.

Following the Threads

Following conversations in a chatroom can prove a lot more challenging than on posting boards, which remain static and can be sifted through systematically.

In a real-time chat, each person's posting, which makes up the conversation, scrolls onto the screen in one of three ways:

1. instantly as the person types it (this was more common when text-based BBSs were in use)
2. near-immediate, so it shows up in full after the person hits Return or Send (this is the most common way)
3. after a webpage refreshes at regular intervals or when you manually refresh or "reload" the page, which is the case of some World Wide Web–based chatrooms

The most common rhythm of an online chat on both commercial online services and many websites that use special chat software is the near-immediate way, with messages appearing on the screen as quickly as people can type and hit Return.

When you have only a few people in the room, chances are the conversation is all-inclusive, so everyone is participating in the same conversation and the delays are only as the others wait politely for someone to finish his or her thought. But most chatrooms are chaotic, with many conversations going on at the same time.

Chat Quick Tips

Say Their Name: Always address the person you are speaking to by name, that is, the individual's userid or screen name or an obvious abbreviation of it. This helps the other person notice when you are speaking to him or her directly and helps other people see that a conversation is in place. Some examples of abbreviating names:

GIRL673 can become Girl
JoeSmith can become Joe
Cybergrrl can become Cyber

Keep It Short: Most chatrooms have limits to the number of characters you can fit into the "box" or "field" where you type your message before posting or sending. Learn to keep your sentences brief, to the point, and friendly. If you have a lot to say and think you will exceed the character limit, type an ellipsis at the end of your phrase and continue. For example, first post:

```
Hi, I was wondering what everyone was talking
about . . .
```

Second post:

```
and I'd like to join the conversation.
```

Note that in an unmoderated chat, other people will continue to post and speak, but anyone paying attention to you knows that you are still talking by the ". . ." at the end of each line.

Don't Use Caps: When you use all capital letters in an email or anywhere on the Internet, for that matter, it means that you are SHOUTING, and it is considered rude and obnoxious. Often, using all caps is the sign of a new user, and if you use them, you are opening yourself up to being criticized or flamed.

The wrong way to "speak" in chat is:

```
Well, I spend most of my time in my garden where I
grow vegetables such as carrots, peas, squash, and
tomatoes and I also have a flower garden where I
have prize roses and then other times I cook and
bake homemade breads.
```

The right way to chat is:

```
I love gardening—vegetable and flower (won
prizes)—and baking. I make great homemade breads.
```

If you are a fast typist, you could do this. First post:

```
Well, I spend most of my time in my garden where I
grow vegetables such as carrots, peas, squash, and
tomatoes . . .
```

Second post:

```
and I also have a flower garden where I have prize
roses and then other times I cook and bake
homemade breads.
```

Face it, in chat, you don't want to sound long-winded, and the conversation could change two or three times before you even got the second posting out.

Another way to be brief is to use acronyms.

Some Common Net Acronyms

BTW	By the way
LOL, ROFL	Laugh out loud, roll on the floor laughing
IMO, IMHO	In my opinion, in my humble opinion
FYI	For your information
RL, IRL	Real life, in real life
FWIW	For what it's worth
TIA	Thanks in advance
WRT	With regard to
WYSIWYG	(Pronounced "Wizzywig") What you see is what you get
RTFM	Read the "f-ing" manual (commonly used by someone who is impatient with a person who hasn't read the FAQ or instructions—yes, this is an insult or "flame")

Show Emotions (Sparingly): Any time you are relying on the digital word to convey a thought or feeling, you're bound to discover the interesting limitations of lacking body language or facial expressions. Regardless of where you post your messages online (posting board, chatroom, email), keep in mind that the reader of your message might not get your sarcasm without your wry smile or chuckle.

Also, as you keep your message brief, chances are you might sound abrupt or cold. So learn to infuse your conversation with occasional emotional cues. Some of these cues can simply be an expression or body gesture typed between <> or ::, such as <grin>, <blush>, or ::Moving across the room to grab a soda::.

You can also use symbols to represent actions; these are called **Emoticons**. Beware of Emoticon-itis, which is the annoying habit of overusing smileys and other symbols. One or two emoticons (or no emoticons) per post is about the maximum anyone else can tolerate.

Think of too many smileys this way: Try smiling a wide, toothy grin from ear to ear after every sentence in a face-to-face conversation. Pretty crazy, right?

Look at most of the following emoticons sideways, with the colon on top and parentheses on the bottom, to see what they symbolize:

:) or :-)	Smiley, happy, grin (the latter is a smiley with a nose)
;-)	Wink, just kidding, it's a joke
:-/	Errr, ambivalence
:-]	Smirk
:-D	Big smile
8-)	Wide-eyed
:-X	Closemouthed
:-P	Sticking tongue out
:-O	Surprise, scream
:-(or =-(	Sad, long face
:-*	Blowing a kiss
>:-)	Pointy eyebrows indicate mischievousness
:->	Pointy smile can also indicate mischievousness, tight grin
{{()}}	Hug and you can personalize it by putting a person's name between brackets

Emoticons vary, and you can certainly create your own, but you may have to explain them when you first use them. See http://www.netsurf.org/~violet/Smileys/ for Pierre Violet's List of Smileys.

Be Nice: The minute you overstep any boundaries of politeness or good taste, you open the entire chatroom to unnecessary fighting, bickering, and flaming. Remember the Golden Rule? Well, doing unto others as you'd like them to do unto you is the perfect rule to follow when you are communicating online, particularly in chatrooms.

Learn to "Read" Chat: The way to read a chatroom is to scan quickly from top to bottom and focus only on the conversation threads that interest you or that are being held between people you know. You'll learn how to jump to only the postings from the person or people with whom you are having a conversation even if there are ten other conversations going on at the same time.

Keep in mind that each chatroom displays only a certain number of messages on the screen at once, usually with new messages posting at the top of the screen and old messages disappearing from the bottom. Some chatrooms allow you to increase or decrease the number of messages showing. Some rooms post more quickly than others. You'll have to learn the features and rhythm of each chatroom to most effectively follow or carry on a conversation in an unmoderated chatroom.

Chatters and Lurkers

In every chatroom, as in every party or social setting, you have the good conversationalists, the conversation monopolizers, and the wallflowers, or "lurkers" as they are known online. Most chatrooms have a way to identify who else is in the room with you, usually by displaying their userid or screen name and sometimes offering a feature where you can display their personal profile, which they might have filled out on the service to better identify themselves. See Chapter 8 for safety tips about personal profiles.

Good chatters keep the conversation moving, engaging others in the chatroom in discussion and greeting new people as they enter the chatroom. Lurkers are the ones who usually don't say a word but are simply "listening in" on the conversation. Lurking is also a good way to get a feeling for the "room" and the kind of people participating.

Before speaking in any chatroom, it is always good to get a feel for the environment. Like any online community, live chat often involves people who visit the chatroom regularly and know the other chatters. When entering a chatroom, imagine that you've walked into a social setting and conversations are going on among people who know one another. Lurking is similar to standing in the background as you listen for the right moment to say something, even if it's just hello.

Don't just lurk! Get out there and socialize!

The Moderated Chat

Some online services have scheduled chat events on specific topics or with special guests—authors, actors, and experts in a particular field. Moderated chats are led by a host or moderator who directs the conversation in a more organized fashion. On America Online, for example, you can attend a regular chat on women's issues on Tuesday nights hosted by EvaS (see Chapter 13 for her profile). When you enter the chatroom, you immediately see a message letting you know the topic or that evening's guest and then another message will explain the rules of a moderated chat.

A fully moderated chat can mean that you should not speak out of turn; in order to speak, you often have to type a ? if you have a question or an ! if you have a comment and then the moderator will call on you to speak. Helpful hint: Type the beginning of your question or comment in the message field but do not hit Send. When the moderator calls on you, hit Send so that the first part of your post is sent right away and you have time to type the rest while people are reading the first one.

Some moderated chats use special software so that your questions or comments are actually sent to the moderator and not to the chatroom until they are approved. Or the moderator might paraphrase your post and ask the question or make the comment on your behalf. Moderators can also use their discretion not to post your message at all. An example of a chatroom that uses special software to be fully moderated is the America Online auditorium in AOL Live.

Moderated chats can be very useful and more enjoyable than the looser chats because you can usually follow the conversation and tend to get more directed information. Very large moderated chats, however, can make you feel more like a lurker than a participant, but you can be in the audience of a chat with top celebrities such as Rosie O'Donnell.

Taking a Chat Private

When in a chatroom, you might get a private message, sometimes called an instant or quick message. On America Online, the instant message is accompanied by a distinctive bell to let you know you've been "IM'd." Instant messages are private between you and the other person who has signaled you. Sometimes the other person is interested in asking you more specific questions. Other times the person will invite you to chat privately. Most services allow you to block instant messages, and you can also ignore them.

Many chatrooms have a feature where you can create your own private room. Private chatrooms are great when you create them to talk among friends. I remember when my sister moved to Santa Fe and I was in New York City, she used to call me and say, "Go online. Go to 'puppy' chatroom." We'd both log on to AOL and create a room, call it puppy or some other simple name, and then we'd chat online. We could chat for an hour for a fraction of the cost of any long-distance phone call.

When a stranger invites you into a private chatroom, use your discretion. Follow the safety tips given in Chapters 8 and 9 to make sure you don't end up in an uncomfortable situation. Keep in mind that some people engage in "cybersex" online in chatrooms. The easiest way to describe cybersex is to compare it to "talking dirty" on the telephone. Instead of verbally describing sexual acts, participants type the descriptions. These activities are almost always played out in a private chatroom that is behind "virtual closed doors," so unless you choose to enter a private room, chances are your chat encounters in public rooms will be pretty harmless.

If you do encounter trouble in a chatroom, most services have policies and a method of reporting anyone who "breaks the rules," so make a note of the person's screen name, check his or her profile, and save that information, then forward a report to the administrator of the service you are using. Often, you can log a discussion in a chatroom, a feature you'll find in the menu at the top of your screen. See Chapter 9 for more tips on reporting inappropriate behavior online.

The Internet Chat—IRC

IRC, or Internet relay chat, is the chat function on the Internet rather than on a closed commercial online service. IRC was first meant for users on a BBS (bulletin board system) to chat amongst themselves. Now IRC supports a worldwide network of servers, so it is available to anyone with an Internet connection and the right software. IRC is a text-only conferencing system that works in real time, and each topic-related chatroom in IRC is called a **channel**. You have to log into an IRC server such as Undernet (http://www.undernet.org) in order to access the IRC channels such as #help.

IRC software includes Ircle (http://www.shadowmac.org/pub/mirrors/Info-Mac/Internet/ircle-25.hqx) or Homer (http://www.shadowmac.org/pub/mirrors/Info-Mac/_Internet/ homer-094.hqx) for Macs and mIRC (http://www.mirc.com/) for PCs.

Other sources of free or cheap Internet tools software include Jumbo (http://www.jumbo.com) and Shareware.com (http://www.shareware.com). (These are all websites where you can download software onto your computer. For more details about the Web, see Chapter 6.)

From Lana Vyte, elementary school teacher, single
mother

I have been using IRC six months or so to
alleviate feelings of isolation. I spend most of
my evenings housebound. This is a conscious choice
as I prefer to be available to my son, especially
on weeknights. Also, for the single mother living
in the far reaches of suburbia, going out for
social and other events calls for planning,
preparation, and money. Then there are some nights
when I'm just too tired to put in the effort of
getting ready or preparing for guests.

Internet Relay Chat provides the perfect solution
for me. In cyberspace no one knows what you look
like or how you're dressed. You can be sick with
the flu or in your nightie. You can enter and
leave numerous chatrooms effortlessly and with a
minimum fuss or excuse; talk with whomever you
please; make new friends and even party. Distance
and time take a back seat. Socializing is quick,
easy, and oh-so-convenient.

Some nights I am online past midnight, talking
and laughing and just generally having a wonderful
time with so many people, all from the safety
and comfort of my own den. I don't go to just
one party—I go to many and I've made friends whom
I have met in real life as well. It's a great way
to expand a social circle and lessen feelings of
isolation no matter where you are.

My son, Ramon, is likewise catching the "bug."
He comes home from school and hooks up to Kidlink
to talk with his "cyberbuddies" and keep in touch
with friends who have moved away. He loves it
and his keyboarding and spelling skills have

certainly improved. IRC has become a part of
our lives.

Chatting on the Web

When websites first became popular, their main feature was
to link pages of information. Posting boards on websites were
primitive at best and there wasn't really chat but rather a link that
launched into IRC on the Internet. But as businesses began
looking to the Web, new features were developed and webchat
began appearing.

Some webchats that deliver a real-time feeling require either
plug-ins, which are mini-software programs that you need to
download from the Web onto your computer so your Web
browser can launch into chat, or the webchat is driven by Java, a
type of computer language and process that can only be activated
by an enhanced browser, such as Netscape 3.0 and Internet Explorer 3.0 or higher.

Other webchats use what are called cgi scripts to push information to your Web browser to reload or refresh the Web page
so you can see the new chat messages or post your own message
onto the page. These webchats are a little slower than commercial
online service chats or the webchats with plug-ins or Java.

Websites are adding chat and posting board features to their
sites to create a sense of "place" on the site, rather than a resource for information that is just read. Successful websites add
"interactivity" to emulate the commercial online services, which
attract subscribers who become a part of a "community," which
keeps them coming back time and time again.

Communicating in Communities

Online communities have their own set of rules, sometimes
written in FAQs (a list of frequently asked questions), but often
unspoken rules that everyone just seems to know, except per-
haps you, as a "newbie" online. "Newbie" is the term given to

people who have recently come online by those who have been online for some period of time.

Being new online can be disorienting at best, utter chaos and confusion at worst, but if you approach going online as an adventure and realize that as long as you "read the signs"—that is, read posts and email with care and use proper Net etiquette in the way you act and react—you will find online communities quite welcoming.

Net+Etiquette = Netiquette

Wrapup

People use posting boards, bulletin boards, or message boards to leave messages for each other online. Usenet newsgroups are text-based message boards on the Internet. There is also the same type of posting board on commercial online services.

Threaded messaging boards have several ongoing conversations, or "threads," happening simultaneously. To learn more about the board you are viewing, read its FAQ (frequently asked questions) file. If you don't follow the rules of the posting board and are not polite or ask questions that have been answered a hundred times, you risk being flamed or insulted by other people who post to the board.

Internet mailing lists are like message boards except that all postings come directly to your email box. You can choose to subscribe to the digest version of the mailing list to consolidate all of the postings into a few emails so you don't get too many emails at once. Lists might be moderated or unmoderated (monitored or open) by the person or people who run the list.

Chat online is carried out in chatrooms where many people gather and "talk" to each other by typing what they want to say. When they hit Return or Enter on their keyboard or click a button to Send or Speak, their words are posted in the room pretty much instantly for everyone in the chatroom to see.

Communicating on the Internet can be done in many different ways, but regardless of how you choose to communicate online, safety should always be your number one concern. Let's find out ways to make sure that our time online is hassle-free.

part three

WHO'S AFRAID OF THE "BIG, BAD 'NET"

Chapter 8   Online Safety Tips

Forget what you've read about the Internet being a dangerous place, or at least read it all with a good dose of skepticism. The first thing to remember about the Internet is that it is simply another way to communicate. The next thing to remember is that it is a direct reflection of the world in which we live—good and bad.

Let's explore some of the Myths of the Internet and dispel them once and for all.

Myth 1: Now that I've connected my computer to a commercial online service or the Internet, horrible hackers will be able to get inside my computer and steal my information or damage my hard drive.

Fact: Now what kind of information do you have on your personal computer that would really interest a hacker? The reality is that when your modem dials out and connects with America Online or Prodigy or to the Web through an Internet service provider (ISP), you are not opening your computer to invasion. You are performing a closed communications function. The only computers that are potential targets for hackers are the ones that are dedicated to the Internet twenty-four hours a day, seven days a week—those computers that are always on and always connected. Those computers usually install security systems to protect their data and block unauthorized access.

Myth 2: The Net is made up of criminals, thieves, and perverts, all waiting for me to log on so they can hurt me, rob me, and harass me.

Fact: If the Net is like a big city of over 20 million people, chances are most of them don't have time to zero in on you as their next prey. Enter this new electronic city with intelligence, awareness, and the proper netiquette, and your chances of becoming an online victim are greatly reduced.

Myth 3: I have no control over what happens to me on the Internet. If someone "sees" me online, they can find me and come after me. If they harass me, I have nowhere to go.

Fact: You have more control over your safety online. You have to be aware of the ways that you can protect your identity. You can make choices about what information you reveal to someone online. And if someone is bugging you, you can always turn off the computer. If they persist and you feel that things have gotten out of hand, you can change your account name or email address. See Chapter 9 for ways to deal with the online pest.

So how can we all be cyber–street smart and prevent unwanted advances from those few folks who might be lurking in the shadows of the Big Bad Net? Here are some basic ways to keep you and your family safer when surfing the Net.

Choose Your Screen Name Wisely

You may want to use initials and abbreviations for your name rather than your full name both when registering for your online account and when picking your screen name. That way you aren't revealing your identity or gender the minute you enter a chatroom or post a message and can retain a bit of privacy until you feel comfortable enough to disclose further information.

Keep in mind that with many Internet accounts, your registration information is available if someone decides to "finger" you (an online technique whereby anyone can access a file of basic information about you). Therefore, ask your Internet provider beforehand that your phone number and address not be included in this finger file, or find out how you can edit it right away. On commercial online services, this is usually called your profile.

Keep Personal Information Private

Eventually, you may feel comfortable enough to reveal your full name or other bits of personal and possibly identifying information to someone you encounter on the Net, but use the same discretion that you would use if you met a total stranger on the street—and maybe a little more.

Would you walk up to someone in New York City and say "Hi, my name is Jane Doe, I live at 123 Main Street, and by the way, here's my phone number and credit card number, too."? I don't think so! So why would you give any of this information out online? Even if someone approaches you online and claims to be an "official" of the commercial online service or your service provider, refrain from telling anything. Official employees of these services do not ask for personal information online, period.

Personal Profiles—the Safe Way

Many online services allow you to post information about yourself that can be retrieved by other members of the service. A good thing to remember is to check the Profile feature the first day you log into the service, because often it will automatically contain some basic information about yourself, pulled from the initial application you filled out when you signed up. On the Internet, this profile is called your finger file and you should ask your ISP how to access and edit your finger file so you can delete any information you do not want to make public.

Safe Info for Profiles
1. First name
2. State or country
3. Hobbies, interests
4. A favorite quote

Questionable Info for Profiles
1. City where you live (As long as you don't include your last name, this could be okay.)
2. Sex (Only include if you are prepared to be approached online either via instant messages, chat, or email based on

whether you are male or female. Most services have the option for "no comment" or another neutral response.)

3. P.O. box (Some people feel safe using a P.O. box address online in case someone wants to send something via "snailmail" or regular postal service; however, people can still track down who you are if they know your P.O. box or they can send you inappropriate things.)

4. Voicemail number (Having a voicemail number separate from your home can also give a false sense of security since you can also be tracked down if someone really wants to find you that way.)

5. Age (Unless you feel it is essential to reveal your age to anyone who wants to know, it's best to keep this your own private information. Some forums require that you identify your age if they are age-specific, especially for kids or seniors.)

Do *Not* Include in Profiles

1. Last name
2. Location address
3. Social security number
4. Phone number
5. Credit card or bank account numbers

Online Security—Is Your Credit Card Safe?

For the record, it is safer for you to enter your credit card number into the database of an online service or on an ordering form through a website than having your credit card in your purse or wallet. It is more common for the carbons of your credit card transaction to be lifted in a store than to have your credit card number intercepted while you are buying something online.

I'm not saying that there aren't occasions when a hacker steals credit card numbers from someone online, but the two most common ways are:

1. Breaking into the computer system of a small online service and stealing all of the credit card numbers of the subscribers. If you ever read the news stories about Kevin Mitnick, the big hacker who was caught, this is how he stole thousands of credit card numbers.

2. Getting the credit card numbers simply by asking the credit card holder for them. This may sound ridiculous, but many people actually give their credit card numbers to total strangers online when asked, such as on a commercial online service or via email. Remember that a legitimate business will never ask for your credit card number through chat, instant messaging, or email.

The worst thing that can happen to you if someone "steals" your credit card number is that you will see charges on your credit card that you don't recognize. If this happens, call your credit card company; you might be responsible for up to $50 of that charge. Hackers usually won't bother to use your credit card number more than once for fear of getting caught.

When you visit a website where you can shop online, you are usually notified by your browser when you are entering a "secure transaction" area. You may get a box popping up on your browser that says this and you just click "okay," or if you are using Netscape Navigator, you'll see the tiny yellow broken key at the bottom left corner of your browser suddenly turn into a solid key.

Reputable stores on the Web have spent the extra money to make sure their site is **secure** for transactions, which means they have bought special software that **encrypts** or codes the transaction message so your credit card is protected.

For some great places to shop online, check out Chapter 12. These sites are Cybergrrl Approved for quality service and merchandise.

Chapter 9   Netiquette and Dealing with the Online Pest

Half the secret to "staying safe" online has to do with behaving properly, being aware of your "surroundings," and knowing how to respond, or not to respond, to unwanted attention from a stranger. Doesn't this sound just like the advice your mother gives you when you visit or move to a big city?

Read and Listen Before Speaking Up

When you enter a new chat area or begin reading a Usenet newsgroup, hang out for a while and observe—or "lurk," as this is called. It is okay to do this, especially if you're paying attention to the content of the area, the tone, the topics, and so on. When you think you have a sense of what is appropriate to say, then speak up. And you'll make friends on the Net if, when you speak up, you offer some valuable advice, suggestions, or answers to someone's questions (but only if you know the answer, of course).

Being sensitive to the atmosphere of the community you enter will help you avoid getting flamed or harassed or insulted. Think of your position as similar to walking toward a group of people who know each other and whose conversation has already started. You would probably say "Pardon me, but I couldn't help but overhear . . ." rather than "Hey, I'm new to the Net, and by the way, my company is offering Ginsu knives on sale, but only if you act now and did I mention that I don't know what you're talking about, but I'm going to express my opinion anyway."

Do Unto Others . . .

The Golden Rule applies both in the real world and in cyberspace; after all, everything online is merely an electronic extension of the real world—it is not some foreign, unidentifiable place. The Net is filled with real people, lots of them. If you are rude, chances are people will be rude right back. If you are polite and friendly, the responses you receive online will usually reflect that. Being a nice person on the Net doesn't guarantee you won't ever be harassed, but a little kindness does go a long way.

When you are online, you have a major safety barrier as long as you do not reveal personal information about yourself, including your full name, location, or contact numbers. You are safer behind your computer terminal than on any street in any major city. So go online, meet interesting people, find useful information, and discover the world. Being smart helps you be safe!

Nine times out of ten, an insulting email or a dirty message is an invitation for trouble. But the person on the other end is waiting for you to respond to feed into his or her game. If you ignore these people, chances are they will move on to someone else, because what fun is silence or a blank screen? Chances are, the message you got first was somewhat random, like a crank phone call.

Try to remember to record the name of the offender or save the message onto your hard drive. On a closed system like a commercial online service, you can use this as evidence when you file a report to its complaint or customer service department.

If you are continually harassed, you may have to change your screen name or open a new account on another service, but this is just an annoyance and not a real-world danger. The danger comes in if you respond to the harasser and if you reveal identifying information about yourself or the harasser is able to access it online.

The Legal Issues of Cyberstalking

Victims of cyberstalking—being harassed online through email or other communications methods—have a difficult time proving their case in order to get law enforcement to take action against the harasser. Why do people stalk other people online? Anonymity on the Internet makes it easy for people to act out fantasies or behave in a way they would not in their real-world life.

California was the first state to enact a law making stalking a crime. This law makes it a crime to repeatedly harass or follow another person as well as make a "credible threat" that puts people in reasonable fear for their safety or the safety of their immediate family. Other states have since enacted similar laws or revised their old stalking laws. Only seven of those states, however, deal with stalking by computer (Alaska, Delaware, Connecticut, Michigan, Montana, Oklahoma, and Wyoming). The federal government recently passed an amendment to the Communications Act of 1934, changing the language to include computers as a telecommunications device.

Twenty-one other states have statutes with wording that could be applied in the cyberspace context (including Alabama, California, Colorado, Florida, Georgia, Iowa, Louisiana, Massachusetts, Maryland, Minnesota, New Mexico, Ohio, Tennessee, Texas, Utah, Virginia, Washington, and Wisconsin). The wording includes the act of written communication or the use of the telephone as a tool for harassment. Since written communication is the key to online communication, email fits into the legal requirement of written communication. But since the Internet is a network of computers linked by telephone lines, an argument could be made that technically, email sent through the Internet is a form of telephone communication.

Enforcing laws in cyberspace is a problem law enforcement agencies have never faced before. A major problem is jurisdiction, because since the Internet links people around the world, whose laws would be enforced? If someone in the United States is harassed by someone in Asia, or if both harasser and victim are in the United States but in different states, what are law enforcement agents to do? Which state laws apply: the state where the victim lives or where the harasser lives? In six of the seven states that specify electronic stalking in their statutes, the first offense is considered a misdemeanor (Delaware is the only state that considers it a felony).

One way to get around the problem of jurisdiction could be to prosecute under the federal law that prohibits obscenity or harassment using interstate telecommunications devices. Unfortunately, this doesn't help if the stalker is in another country.

Another problem with prosecuting an online stalker is identity. Often, a cyberstalker uses fake information to get an online account, so he or she cannot be tracked down.

What Do You Have to Prove?

If you feel you are being stalked online, you have to prove it; so make sure you save every piece of evidence of the harassment, including emails, instant messages, attached files, and chatroom transcripts. All of these text-based communications or files can be saved on your hard drive and then saved onto a floppy disc. You must:

1. Prove that there is an intent to harass you, even a "credible threat"—and that the stalker plans to carry out the threat.
2. Prove that the harassment has been made frequently enough to be called a single episode of harassment.
3. Try to establish identification and provide law enforcement with every possible clue to the person's employment, possible residence, and any other personal history and identifying information you may have.

Be aware of the anonymous remailer—an online service on the Internet that anonymously accepts emails and resends them so that all identifying information is stripped out.

Many of the statutes require that a person be in reasonable fear of physical harm. This means stalkers might be able to send harassing email as long as they don't make a threat or imply that they will hurt their victim physically. Often, cyberstalkers harass in a way that is more an annoyance than an actual threat. The harassment can cause victims severe emotional distress, without threatening their physical safety.

Victims have often had previous contact with their harassers and might be able to prosecute them in civil court. If a harasser is known to the victim, it is easier to prosecute, but if they are out of state, it becomes more difficult.

If offensive email is sent over an office network between coworkers, the victim might have a sexual harassment case. The harassment, however, would need to be frequent, severe, and physically threatening and unreasonably hinder work performance to make a hostile environment claim. Since suits can be brought against employers, there is strong incentive for them to stop the harassment by the employee.

Reporting the Pest

When you first subscribed to a commercial online service such as America Online or CompuServe, you had to "read and accept" a terms-of-service document that outlines proper behavior for the service. If you do not behave properly on the service, your account can be terminated.

If you are being harassed on a COS, report your harasser immediately to the customer service or other member service department. The problem should be solved quickly, because these services want to make sure that their customers are satisfied. Ask your service provider about "kill files" or "bozo filters" to block messages from annoying people.

Use common sense. Think twice before starting an online romance. Remember, you are "talking" to total strangers who can misrepresent themselves.

Chapter 10   Blocking the "Bad Stuff"

Filtering Software and Tools

There is a wide range of blocking software available online and in stores, with different levels of "strictness." Net Nanny and Internet Filter are considered to be more liberal and Cyber Patrol and CYBERsitter are much more conservative. Here are some quick bits of information about some of the blocking software available on the market.

Cyber Patrol

Cyber Patrol is filtering software for the PC or Mac that allows parents to make certain times and areas off-limits to their children, block the use of certain words and phrases from email and chatrooms, and prevent children from revealing names, addresses, or other personal data to others online. Online usage can be customized for each user, with different passwords for Headquarters (where the settings are made) and each child. Parents can alter the blocked-site list. It is provided free of charge to AOL, CompuServe, and Prodigy members, but costs $29.95 plus $29.95 per year for others. A free downloadable demo is available at the Microsystems Software Inc. website: http://www.microsys.com/cyber/default.htm. "Cyber Patrol is the Internet filtering software rated the best by industry and leading magazines," says its website.

CYBERsitter

CYBERsitter is software for the PC that lets parents block, block and alert, or simply alert them when their children try to access inappropriate Web and FTP sites' newsgroups, and send or receive certain words and phrases. A blocked-site list cannot be altered. The program can also be set up to log all Internet activity and prevent kids from giving out personal information. The software costs $39.95 and offers free downloadable updates of restricted sites. URL: http://www.solidoak.com.

Cyber Snoop

Cyber Snoop is PC software that monitors and logs online activity so parents can see what their children have been viewing and decide whether to block it partially, entirely, or not at all. Software shuts down and resets itself if someone tries to disable it without a password. Full Internet blocking is optional. Costs $29.95 with no monthly fees. Phone: 800-732-7596. URL: http://pearlsw.com/csnoop/snoop.htm.

The Internet Filter

The Internet Filter is a software program for PCs that surreptitiously monitors Web pages, newsgroups, email, and chat sessions for specific words, phrases, or whole addresses of concern. It is less restrictive than Cyber Patrol or CYBERsitter (allowing gay topics but not gay sex, for example) but can be configured to be stricter if desired. It lets parents choose whether to block or just record offensive areas attempted and even be emailed if their children attempt to gain access to an area of concern. You can download and distribute a free, limited feature version off the website from http://www.turnercom.com or buy the full version for $40. Phone: 604-708-2397.

Net Nanny

Net Nanny software for PCs lets parents monitor, screen, block, and log all computer activity, online or off, including online services, websites, newsgroups, chat, FTPs, email, BBSs, words, phrases, personal information (address, credit card numbers, etc.), local computer files, drives, diskettes, CD-ROMs, and point-and-click commands. Does not offer tailoring of restrictions for individual ages, although parents can use a password to override restrictions when they use the computer. You can download a thirty-day trial version of the software off the website: http://www.netnanny.com. Price is $19.95 if you order online; $39.95 if you order by phone; there are no subscription fees. Phone: 800-340-7177.

Rated-PG

Rated-PG software allows parents to limit access to and time spent on all computer activity, online or off, including CD-ROM games, websites, chat, email, newsgroups, even re-routing email with foul language directly to the parent. Restrictions can be customized to each user, varying according to the maturity and education levels of different children. Software also generates reports of all system activities by child, by site, by game or application, by time and date. Can be ordered by phone (714-553-8883) or fax (714-852-8136) for $54.95. First two updates of X-Rated sites are free, subsequent updates available by subscription for $14.95 per quarter, $29.95 per six months, or $39.95 per year. For more information, visit the website: http://www.ratedpg.com.

Safesearch

Safesearch is filtering software for PCs that controls access to websites, chatrooms, newsgroups, and online service content and offers control of outgoing information so children can't give out credit card numbers, addresses, or phone numbers. Does not filter specific words or phrases. Each user has a different password so access can be individually tailored. If a child wants to enter a restricted area, he or she can get permission from Mom or Dad, who can enter a password to let Junior into that particular site. Software can be downloaded for a free ten-day trial off the website: http://www.safesearch.com. Subscriptions cost $49.95 per year or $29.95 per six months. Phone: 972-424-7882.

SurfWatch

SurfWatch Internet filtering software for PC and Mac screens for newsgroups, websites, FTP, Gopher, chat, and other sites likely to contain sexually explicit material. Does not block individual words in email or chatrooms. Not for use with online services (AOL, CompuServe, Prodigy). Cost: $49.95 per copy. Subscriptions are $5.95 per month. Phone 888-677-9542. URL: http://www.surfwatch.com

X-Stop

X-Stop is software for the PC and Mac that blocks objectionable content on the computer, whether it originates online or with the computer user. Forbids customizable bad words from being typed on the computer. Blocks pornography from WWW, Usenet, FTP sources, adding two hundred sites to its forbidden list every day. Also disables certain words used in search engines to search for pornography on the Internet. ("This is a different library than the 'foul language' filter and includes words that are OK to type ANYWHERE ELSE but the Search Engine Monitor. Example: 'lingerie' in most search engines returns pornography sites, so we block the word.") Costs $39.95, plus $9.00 per year for updates; company offers thirty-day guarantee. For information, visit the company's website at http://www.xstop.com or call 888-STOPXXX.

Be aware that some of these blocking software products are under scrutiny for blocking information that is not necessarily obscene, such as reproductive health information and feminist information.

So now that you've learned a little about online safety, how do you find the information that is relevant to your interests and your life? Let's find out!

part four

MAKING THE WEB WORK FOR YOU

The Web is full of useful (and useless) resources, and there often seems to be no rhyme or reason as to how things are organized or who chooses what is published online and what is not.

So how do you find resources online that are relevant to your life, sites that contain information that is truly useful or simply entertaining? What is on the World Wide Web that makes it worth your time and any effort it might take to get online?

I always say that by going online, you can benefit both professionally and personally, and the only way to prove that statement is to give you some concrete examples of both. Rather than creating an exhaustive list of women's sites on the Web, I've chosen some examples of recommended sites under several categories to give you a taste for what is out there.

Some of the sites in this chapter are specifically geared toward women, while others are more general in their appeal. I may mention but don't list sites for TV shows, magazines, or other things that already exist in the "real world." The sites in the lists here have been created just for the Web and are only available online.

For other topics of interest, visit one of the many searchable directories or search engines on the Web such as Yahoo (http://www.yahoo.com/) or Excite (http://www.excite.com/) to find exactly what you want. (For details, go back to Chapter 6.)

Chapter 11   The Professional You

Career

There are many sites on the Web where you can search through job listings, post your résumé, and find other resources to embark on a new career or help you with your current one.

Career Mosaic
http://www.careermosaic.com/
Find a job almost anywhere in the world using this site's Web and newsgroup databases, job fairs, career tips, and résumé posting service. Employers can post jobs and view candidates' résumés.

CareerPath
http://www.careerpath.com
Search this site's help-wanted database by newspaper, job category, and keyword. Investigate potential employers with the site's profiles of "America's leading employers" with links to corporate sites, jobs, and email.

Cool Jobs
http://www.cooljobs.com
This site posts what it deems "cool jobs," from circus performers to insurance underwriters to professional brewers.

Monster Board
http://www.monsterboard.com
Job seekers can search a worldwide jobs database, use a personal job search agent, post résumés, get career advice, and use the site's relocation services to find housing and other services in their new cities. Employers can post jobs and conduct résumé searches.

Business

For those who currently have businesses, including home-based, there are many useful sites with advice and information for entrepreneurs and executives alike. Keep in mind that many of your favorite business publications such as *Inc.* (http://www.inc.com/), *Home Office Computing* (http://www.hoc.com/), *Fortune* (http://www.fortune.com/), and *Success* (http://www.successmagazine.com/) are also online in addition to those created just for the Web.

Field of Dreams
http://www.fodreams.com/home.html
A site created by and for women in business with sections for a directory, business promotion, website design, advice and info on building your business, and research.

Ideacafe
http://www.ideacafe.com/
Site for small businesses with sections on financing, communications, horoscopes, articles, a Web guide, and so on.

Jane Applegate
http://www.janeapplegate.com/
The Voice of Small Business, syndicated columnist Jane Applegate, offers sound advice for the small business owner.

Small Business Adviser
http://www.isquare.com/
Online information for the entrepreneur and new business owner, from finding capital to dealing with the IRS.

Webgrrls
http://www.webgrrls.com/
Resource for women interested in learning about the Internet or finding a mentor or job in the new media and technology industries.

Women's Connection
http://www.womenconnect.com/

Current news on women's issues (archived for thirty days), bulletin boards, a library covering such topics as business, politics, health, finance, and gender equity, information about women's organizations, links to women's sites on the Web, and a regionalized events calendar.

Working Solo
http://www.workingsolo.com/

This site offers business advice for entrepreneurs, including an online database of resources for entrepreneurs, articles, book reviews, books and tapes, and a newsletter.

FedEx
http://www.fedex.com/

Use this site to track packages, find out rates and drop-off locations, arrange for a pickup, and sign up for an account.

UPS
http://www.ups.com/

And you can track your UPS packages, too. Very handy!

Finance

Check stocks, learn more about saving for your retirement, access financial and business sites for *The Wall Street Journal* (http://www.wsj.com/), *Money* magazine (http://www.money.com/), the New York Stock Exchange (http://www.nyse.com/), and more.

EDGAR
http://www.sec.gov/edgarhp.htm

EDGAR—the Electronic Data Gathering, Analysis, and Retrieval system—performs automated collection, validation, indexing, acceptance, and forwarding of submissions by companies and others who are required by law to file forms with the U.S. Securities and Exchange Commission (SEC).

Fidelity Investments
http://personal.fidelity.com/
Information on personal investing, workplace savings, and using a financial adviser.

Merrill Lynch
http://www.ml.com/isb/isbfra.htm
Finances for individuals and small businesses. Includes a Family Savings Center to teach everyone in the family how to save. You can order the company's women's investment handbook at http://www.plan.ml.com/products_services/womenguide.html.

Quicken Financial Network
http://www.qfn.com/
Retirement planning and debt reduction, stock and mutual fund quotes, rates on personal loans, credit cards, and savings accounts, and insurance quotes.

Taxes

IRS Electronic-Filing System
http://www.irs.ustreas.gov/plain/elec_svs/ol-txpyr.html
You have to install software and still mail in a hard copy of your IRS forms (just in case), but here you can file your tax forms online and get a direct-deposit refund into your bank account within about three weeks.

Turbo Tax Center
http://www.intuit.com/turbotax/
Created by Intuit, Inc., the company that makes the most popular finance software, this site lets you file your 1040EZ online and has lots of tax-related tips.

Tax Site Directory
http://www.taxsites.com
A more advanced list of the best tax resources on the Internet.

Chapter 12   The Personal You

Websites can also be fun, interesting, or helpful to you for your personal life. You can access the entertainment sites for what you like on television, such as the *Rosie O'Donnell Show* (http://www.rosieo.com/) or Lifetime TV (http://www.lifetimetv.com/). You can visit sites for your favorite authors such as Sue Grafton (http://www.suegrafton.com). You can find sites related to your favorite consumer products, from Tide (http://www.tide.com/) or Pampers (http://www.pampers.com/) to Lee Jeans (http://www.leejeans.com) or Clinique (http://www.clinique.com/).

Websites can impart valuable medical and health information, such as breast cancer information at Avon's Breast Cancer Awareness Crusade Online (http://www.avoncrusade.com/), and domestic violence information, such as SafetyNet Domestic Violence Resources (http://www.cybergrrl.com/planet/dv).

Many websites allow you to reserve a room at a hotel with Ramada (http://www.ramada.com/) or at a Holiday Inn (http://www.holidayinn.com/). And don't forget to stop by the airline sites such as USAir (http://www.usairways.com/) and American Airlines (http://www.american-air.com), where you can find the best fares and book a flight.

Health

When you are dealing with something as sensitive as health issues, you'll want to be more careful about verifying where the information is coming from than if you are looking up entertainment gossip. Many hospitals, health-care management companies, pharmaceutical companies, and other known businesses have websites. The following are reputable health sites, but remember: Always see your own physician about any health issues or concerns.

Healthy Ideas
http://www.healthyideas.com/
Herbal remedies, natural healing, general fitness, and other preventive measures toward better health.

Healthy Woman
http://www.healthgate.com/healthy/woman/index.shtml
Articles on various health issues women face with an archive of past issues.

National Alliance of Breast Cancer Organizations
http://www.nabco.org/
Resources about breast cancer, trials, treatments, and support groups as well as a searchable events calendar and an email breast health reminder to let you know when it's time for your next mammogram.

Planned Parenthood Federation
http://www.ppfa.org/
Planned Parenthood, the world's oldest and largest voluntary family planning organization, offers resources on sexual and reproductive health; contraception/birth control/family planning; pregnancy; STDs, including HIV; sexuality education; abortion; pro-choice advocacy; reproductive rights; and Internet links.

Family

Many parents find valuable information and a sense of community at parenting sites where they automatically have kids in common.

Family.com
http://www.family.com/
This site by Disney offers pages with ideas for family activities and outings, recipes, helpful articles on parenting, computing for kids and parents, and creative ideas for learning.

Interactive Pregnancy Calendar
http://www.olen.com/baby/
Program a day-by-day customized calendar to chart the development of a baby from conception to birth.

ParentSoup
http://www.parentsoup.com/
An online community for parents, with advice, chat, polls, and fun.

ParentTime
http://www.parenttime.com/
Gives personalized articles and features based on the age of your child.

Relationships

Personals
Match.com
http://www.match.com/
Online matchmaking for those who are tired of blind dates and the bar scene. Run by Fran Maier of Match.com.

Swoon
http://www.swoon.com/
About dating, mating, and relating with personals, chat, horoscopes, forums, and contests.

Weddings
American Bridal Registry
http://www.abregistry.com/
A free online registry. You can list whatever you want, and then people can come and find out more about the "happy couple" and search their registry.

Plan A Wedding Budget Estimate
http://www.planawedding.com/form.html
Input the estimated dollar amount you want to spend and this site

will give you an idea of how to allocate your funds for everything from attire to transportation to the honeymoon.

BridalNet
http://www.bridalnet.com

A registry, wedding services information, travel tips, and a special "Trippin' Down the Aisle" section to relieve your prewedding stress.

Internet Wedding Links Global Search FIND Page
http://netdreams.com/awedding/search.html

A wedding search engine where you can search by business, by category, or by country.

The Knot
http://www.theknot.com/

A fun guide to wedding information from garters and rings to finding the perfect honeymoon location.

Way Cool Weddings
http://www.waycoolweddings.com

Learn from the detailed wedding experiences of other couples or share your own wedding planning stories.

Travel

Epicurious
http://travel.epicurious.com/

An in-depth travel site where you can find anything from bargain airfares to the weather at your travel destination.

Executive Woman's Travel Network
http://www.delta-air.com/womenexecs

Reserve a flight, plan your itinerary, join a mailing list to receive email about special events or participate in a forum.

GORP
http://www.gorp.com/
Has information on and organizes outdoor recreational and adventure activities and travel packages, sells travel products and books.

Travelocity
http://www.travelocity.com/
Book your travel reservations, read information about travel destinations, buy merchandise, and get those last-minute travel deals.

Travelgrrl
http://www.travelgrrl.com/
A searchable database of travel stories by women and a forum for women travelers to exchange tips and information. Helps promote women travel writers as well.

Entertainment

Most of the movie studios and record companies have their own websites. You'll even find websites for a particular movie, television show, or recording artist.

General
Eonline
http://www.eonline.com/
From the folks at E! television, this is "Entertainment's Home Page," with news, gossip, reviews, fun and games, a chat area, and special features.

Mr. Showbiz
http://www.mrshowbiz.com/
News, reviews, featured articles, daily headlines, star bios, and fun, interactive games.

Movies

Girls On Film
http://www.girlsonfilm.com/
"Chicks, flicks, and politicks" features articles, movie reviews, and girls' views on everything from books to Kitty Litter.

Hollywood Online
http://www.hollywood.com/
Movie and video guide, celebrity news, and everything you would expect to come from Hollywood.

Movielink
http://www.movielink.com/
Movie information with movie schedules for all theaters in many major cities. You can buy your tickets online for many of these theaters using your credit card. And visit the Movielink Cafe to talk about movies with other people around the world.

Sundance Institute
http://www.sundance.org/
Home of the Sundance Film Festival, "dedicated to the support and development of emerging screenwriters and directors of vision, and to the national and international exhibition of new, independent dramatic and documentary films." Includes a searchable film database.

Music

Ladyslipper.org
http://www.ladyslipper.org/
Ladyslipper is a nonprofit organization whose primary purpose is to heighten public awareness of the achievements of women artists and musicians, and to expand the scope and availability of recordings by women.

Musicgrrl
http://www.musicgrrl.com/
Entertaining site featuring women musicians and female-fronted

bands. Find out what it's like to be a woman in music and what it's really like out on the road.

Sports

Just Sports for Women
http://www.justwomen.com/contents.html
Sports information, services, departments, features, chat, and news—all for women.

Women in Sports
http://www.makeithappen.com/wis/
"Dedicated to providing role models of women athletes that validate women's accomplishments and perpetuate a new vision of women's abilities, autonomy, and self-determination." From rodeos and rugby to skydiving and weight lifting.

Women's Sports by CNN & SI
http://CNNSI.com/womens
Latest news on women's sports from the WNBA to tennis to golf, including highlights from *Womensport* magazine, a special online publication by *Sports Illustrated*.

Food

eGG (Electronic Gourmet Guide)
http://www.foodwine.com/food/egg/
With departments like Just Good Food, the Culinary Sleuth, and the Global Gourmet, this online food magazine also offers a weekly email newsletter.

Epicurious Food
http://food.epicurious.com/
From the publisher of *Gourmet* and *Bon Appetit* magazines. Food, Drink, and "Playing with Your Food," with helpful information on table manners.

Hobbies

Journal of Online Genealogy
http://www.onlinegenealogy.com

A free e-zine (electronic magazine) that focuses on the use of online resources and techniques in genealogy and researching family history.

Home Improvement
http://www.homeideas.com/

The "Ultimate Research Tool for Your Home Project" covering everything from kitchens, baths, paint and wall coverings, lighting and electrical to home decor, heating and cooling, doors and windows, and yard and garden.

Gardening
http://www.gardening.com/

With a plant encyclopedia, answers to over seven hundred plant problems, a garden site directory, and reviews of gardening magazines.

Shopping

Are you worried about buying something online? Are you afraid that entering your credit card number on a website is too risky? See Chapter 8 about online security and breathe easier! So buy those cosmetics at Avon (http://www.avon.com/) or that car at Autobytel (http://www.autobytel.com/) or check out some of these other great shopping sites.

Music

CD Now
http://www.cdnow.com/

Music orders online with weekly specials, daily featured items, buying guides, searches, and contests.

The Music Spot
http://www.musicspot.com/

Music store online with featured artists, discounts, and a helpful customer service.

MusicBoulevard
http://www.musicboulevard.com
VH1 Video shop, MTV CD Lounge, and MB Japan and a shopping catalog of CDs and tapes, along with news and reviews.

Books

Amazon.com
http://www.amazon.com/
Online bookstore with discounted everyday prices and sections for articles, interviews, editor's choice, and a pick of the day.

Barnes & Noble
http://www.barnesandnoble.com/
Bookseller online with a featured index, weekly highlighted subjects, live online events, and a members' area.

Bookstacks Unlimited
http://www.books.com/
Online since 1992, Bookstacks offers some 500,000 titles—most discounted by up to 40 percent! Plus an online reader's community that includes author information, new releases, and book discussions.

Gifts

1-800-Flowers
http://www.1800flowers.com/
Online shopping and gift ideas, events and happenings, contests and fun stuff, an e-zine, floral reference and information, retail stores and opportunities.

Godiva Chocolates
http://www.godiva.com/
Chocolate orders, recipes, gift ideas, seasonal collections, a soap opera, chocolate horoscopes, and an online concierge to make chocolate recommendations.

Computer-related

Cyberian Outpost

http://www.cybout.com/cyberian.html

An online computer mall for the PC or Mac user where you can buy and sell computer goods plus a fun section for kids to check out great toys or meet pen pals.

Internet Shopping Network

http://www.isn.com/

Find a huge selection of the latest computers and computer accessories at bargain prices.

Clothing

J. Crew

http://www.jcrew.com/

Online catalog and orders for paper catalog, men's and women's seasonal clothing, and size chart.

Lands' End

http://www.landsend.com/

Internet clothing store, catalog orders, overstock discounts, swimsuit shop, and biweekly newspaper.

Spiegel

http://www.spiegel.com/

Shopping catalog with additional information for home, work, and play. Links to other stores, including Eddie Bauer, Ultimate Outlet, Spiegeltronics, and Intimate Source.

Good Causes

Although many nonprofit organizations have lacked the funding and resources to build their own website, more and more are finding innovative ways to get online, such as getting a corporation to sponsor their site. If you are interested in giving time or money to a cause, you can use the Web to locate an appropriate organization.

Nonprofit Resources

Foundation Center
http://fdncenter.org/
A site for grant seekers and makers, researchers, policymakers, and the media.

Impact Online
http://www.impactonline.org/
Resources for nonprofit organizations and for the beginning and experienced community volunteer.

Nonprofit Organizations

The Body (AIDS)
http://www.thebody.org/
A comprehensive online resource for learning more about the AIDS virus, where and how to get help and to help others in need.

Envirolink (Environment)
http://envirolink.org/
A grassroots community bringing together worldwide organizations and volunteers to create an extensive environmental resource online.

Girls Incorporated
http://www.girlsinc.org./
A national organization for girls ages six to eighteen that serves largely communities of multiethnic, low-income, and single-parent families.

Seniors

Women and girls aren't the only groups that can benefit from being online. Seniors are going online to find information and to feel connected to others, especially when feeling isolated in their own home or in a retirement home, or when confined to bed or a wheelchair.

AARP (American Association of Retired Persons)
http://www.aarp.org/
Find out about discounts/special offers for the mature citizen or community service programs and much more.

Administration on Aging
http://www.aoa.dhhs.gov/aoa/pages/jpostlst.html
An extensive resource by the government. Not much to look at but useful.

America's Guide: Retirement Living and Senior Care
http://www.americasguide.com/
This site is an extensive guide to senior care facilities across the United States. You can search the database by state and type of facility.

Eldercare Website
http://www.elderweb.com/index.html
A short feature article on the opening page and lots of useful links as you go on. Looks like a good resource.

RetireNet
http://www.retire.net/
With just a simple click into the special pen pal section, hobbies section, chat and other fun stuff, this site is great for the mature adult who is young at heart.

Senior Com
http://www.senior.com/
This site contains information from keeping healthy to traveling inexpensively to Alzheimer's, grieving, and arthritis. There's also a newsstand, a mall devoted to products for seniors, and a "free-store" where you can order complimentary items.

SeniorNet
http://www.seniornet.com
SeniorNet is also a service on America Online and has real-world

SeniorNet Learning Centers across the country. For more information, call 1-800-747-6840 or 415-750-5030.

Women's Resources

Searching for women-specific information online is made easier with two directories specifically for women: Femina (http://www.femina.com/) and WWWomen (http://www.wwwomen.com).

General
Amazoncity
http://www.amazoncity.com/
The first city for women on the Internet complete with Community Square, Health Center, Professional District, Library, and Bazaar, to name just a few.

HomeArts
http://www.homearts.com
The home base for magazines such as *Redbook, Cosmopolitan, House Beautiful, Country Living, Popular Mechanics*, and *Marie Claire*.

Pleiades
http://www.pleiades-net.com/
Pleiades Networks is a place for women to convene and share ideas in a comfortable and engaging environment. Their goal is to create a community of women who share their knowledge and experience to help each other learn and grow as individuals.

Women's Link
http://www.womenslink.com/
Bristol-Myers Squibb's cyberclub for women, where you'll find information on personal care, health, beauty, nutrition, and motherhood designed to help you be your best.

WomensNet
http://www.igc.apc.org/womensnet/
Articles and information by WomensNet, a company that sup-

ports women's organizations worldwide by providing and adapting telecommunications technology to enhance their work.

Feminism
Feminist Activist Resources
http://www.igc.apc.org/women/feminist.html
This guide connects feminist activists to resources on the Internet that are useful and informative.

Feminist.com
http://www.feminist.com/
Complete resources on a wide range of topics concerning women, including activism, women-owned businesses, health issues, articles and speeches, classifieds, and so on.

Feminist Majority
http://www.feminist.org
Unlimited resources for feminists on the Web including research, news and events, a career center, online store, entertainment, 911 for women, university network, and more.

NOW (National Organization for Women)
http://www.now.org/
NOW has a quarter of a million members and hundreds of chapters, which organize protests on issues such as violence against women and abortion rights. They champion new laws and advocate for survivors of rape, sexual harassment, and sex discrimination.

Things to Read

Online publications
GeekGirl
http://www.geekgirl.com.au/geekgirl/
Provocative publication based in Australia featuring women in technology, new media, and women's issues.

gURL
http://www.gurl.com/
A humorous yet realistic look at issues of sexuality, emotions, and body image for young women fourteen years of age and up.

Maximag
http://www.maximag.com/
An urban woman's online magazine with news and forums.

NrrdGrrl
http://www.nrrdgrrl.com/
A gathering place for women who think, talk, and act for themselves with articles, stories, and poetry.

Women's Wire
http://www.women.com/
A well-rounded magazine for the woman interested in fashion, news, entertainment, careers, health, and personal finance.

WomenZone
http://www.womenzone.com/
Articles and conversation for women about issues that concern them from health to careers to humorous looks at fashion.

Education and Learning

American Association of University Women
http://www.aauw.org
This group promotes education and equity for women and girls through research, fellowships and grants, activism, and support for sex discrimination lawsuits.

Artemis Guide to Women's Studies Programs in the United States
http://www.interport.net/~kater/
A resource listing women's studies programs at colleges across the United States.

Feminist Fairytales
http://www.wp.com/dragontree/fairy.html
Encourages educators to use these stories in any (nonprofit or low-profit) way. You're welcome to xerox, put in news-letters, read aloud, dramatize, tape a storytelling session—as long as you include the copyright information and don't change the stories.

Women's History in Archival Collections
http://www.utsa.edu/Library/Archives/links.htm
A guide to websites of archives, libraries, and other resources that have primary source materials by or about women.

General Helpful Web Resources

Email on the Web
Cybergrrl Village
http://village.cybergrrl.com/
Join the Cybergrrl Village, a web-based online service with your own email box to send and receive email both inside the Village and anywhere on the Internet. All you need is Web access to use your Cybergrrl email. Note: You have to register to get your password.

Hotmail
http://www.hotmail.com/
Hotmail is the world's only Web-based free email. It is based on the premise that email access should be easy and possible from any computer connected to the World Wide Web.

Bigfoot
http://www.bigfoot.com/
Bigfoot offers "email for life" where you can consolidate your emails all to be delivered to this Web-based email service.

Lists
The List
http://www.thelist.com

This site provides you with a list of Internet service providers around the country with services, pricing, and contact information.

List of Gender-Related Mailing Lists
http://research.umbc.edu/~korenman/wmst/forums.html
A very comprehensive list of Internet mailing lists covering women-specific topics from health to computer science and everything in between.

List of Newsgroups
http://www.cis.ohio-state.edu:80/
hypertext/faq/usenet
If you are trying to find a newsgroup to suit your interests, stop by this site to find an Internet community on the topic of your choice.

Liszt
http://www.liszt.com/
Searchable list of 65,000 discussion lists and newsgroups.

For the New User
Geocities
http://www.geocities.com
You can establish your own homestead or website here for *free*.

Planet Cybergrrl
http://www.cybergrrl.com/planet/
Let Cybergrrl be "Your guide to the Web, the World, and Life" with Cybergrrl Questions and Answers, Guides to Life, and even an Internet and Web Tutorial and the basics of creating your own website.

Zen and the Art of the Internet
http://www.itec.suny.edu/SUNY/DOC/internet/zen.html
Text version of a booklet that can be used for reference and also gives a foundation about the Internet.

Safe Computing

Anatomy of the Hand and Carpal Tunnel

http://www.scoi.com/handanat.htm

Information about the debilitating affects of carpal tunnel syndrome (CTS) or repetitive stress injury (RSI) and how to treat and prevent them.

The Repetitive Stress Injury Page

http://www.engr.unl.edu/ee/eeshop/rsi.html

Explanation of how typing on a keyboard, dragging a mouse, and other repetitive physical movements can cause injury and ways to prevent it.

Getting the Software (Free or Cheap)

Filemine

http://www.filemine.com/

Has games, multimedia programs, educational software, commercial demos, and more—all of which you can download for free.

Jumbo

http://www.jumbo.com/

Download network with over 200,000 free programs including desktop publishing, games, and homework helpers.

Shareware.com

http://www.shareware.com/

Download the latest software or read up on the site highlights, new arrivals, and most popular selections, by the people at CNET, the television show about technology and the website at http://www.cnet.com.

For the Savvy Net User—Tech News

News.com

http://www.news.com/

Update on technology news on the web.

TechWeb
http://www.techweb.com/
Daily news and features, finance, games, shareware, product reviews, encyclopedia, and more.

Wired.com
http://www.wired.com/
Top stories, updated daily, and special features on business, culture, technology, politics, stocks, and so on.

Finding People
Big Book
http://www.bigbook.com/
Like the Yellow Pages, only online.

Four11
http://www.four11.com/
Another directory for finding people online.

Finding Places
Mapquest
http://www.mapquest.com/
Chart out your road trips with these automatic customized maps, including door-to-door driving directions.

City.net
http://www.city.net/indexes/top_maps.dcg
Another site to create maps to your travel destinations.

part five

THEN THERE WAS WOMAN . . .

What Do Women Want Online?

"Make it useful."
  "Save me time or money . . . or both!"
  "Make it easy to use so it just works."
  "Show me how it fits into my life."
People have definite expectations about what the Internet should be, what it should do for them, and how it looks, feels, and is accessed. Women, who tend to be juggling multiple roles in their lives—mother, partner, career woman—find having to sit down and learn something that seems so technical and complicated to be as inviting as a root canal.

If you look at the Internet as a communications and information tool like the telephone, fax machine, or library card catalog, you begin to get a sense that the computer is just the means to a different kind of end. The Internet is not about computing, it's about connecting—and women want to connect to both people and information when they go online.

I did an informal survey on my Femina website (http://www.femina.com/) asking women for their age, educational background, and income level as well as for information about what they want online.

The results clearly show that women are predominantly doing research and communicating online, and that like the general "picture" of the typical person who is connected online, she is mostly well educated and earning a pretty good salary or living in a household where she has access to computers.

Cybergrrl Survey of Women Online 1995★
Population: 1,150 women surveyed from September 15, 1995, to October 15, 1995

Age: 62% between 18 and 35 years of age; 25% between 36 and 45 years

Education: 64% at least some college, in college, or bachelor's; 29% master's or Ph.D.

★©1995 Cybergrrl, Inc.

Salary: 24% still in school; 34% earn $20,000 to $40,000 per year; 22% over $40,000 per year

Length of Time Online: 47% less than a year; 34% 1 to 3 years

Main Reason for Going Online:

research	33%
email	30%
other (includes browsing, reading news)	23%
community (includes chatting and posting)	13%
shopping	1%

Harassment: 74% say they have never been harassed online

I deliberately asked women if they had been harassed online because, after reading all of the media hype about safety online, harassment, and stalkers, I wanted to know what women were actually experiencing on the Internet. While 74 percent said they had never been harassed online, what was most interesting was that the 26 percent who responded yes described the incidents as more annoyance than actual stalking.

Every woman seems to have a different definition of harassment and even, it seems, a different tolerance level for annoying behavior. Only a handful of women who described their encounters with online harassment actually had to take action, such as reporting the incidents to authorities (their online service providers). Only a few women reported changing their email addresses or contacting the police.

How Many Women Are There?

The number of women online has more than tripled in less than two years, as you can see in the diagram on page 146.

Clearly, there are women using the Internet and the Web for both personal and professional reasons. I'd love to introduce you to some of them.

GROWTH OF WOMEN ON THE WEB

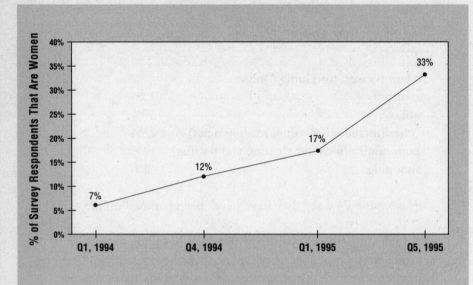

Source: GVU WWW User Surveys, 1995, 1996

Chapter 13   Online Pioneers: The Interviews

Back in the early days—as in just a few years ago—the Internet was truly considered the "wild, wild west." Those who were the first to go online were the scientists and government and military types, followed by academics.

A few brave women began to see the online medium as an opportunity and staked a claim on the uncharted territory not only to make a name for themselves within the online world but also to pave the way for other women who would follow.

Stacy Horn, Forty

http://www.echonyc.com/

Q. *What is your official title and what do you do?*
A. Founder. I run Echo, an online service based in New York City.

Q. *What sites/forums/services are you responsible for creating—that is, what are the highlights of your career?*
A. I started Echo, New York's first virtual community. I've written a book that tells the story of the beginning and evolution of Echo that is coming out from Warner Books in January 1998. It's called *Cyberville: Clicks, Culture, and the Creation of an Online Town.* It's a bizarro *Our Town* in cyberspace kind of tale.

Q. *What is your educational background?*
A. BFA from Tufts University and the School of the Museum of Fine Arts. Master's in Interactive Telecommunications from the Interactive Telecommunications Program at NYU.

Q. *How were you first exposed to computers and what was your initial reaction to them?*
A. It was between a job selling jewelry at Tiffany's and a job

learning about computers. This was 1981. I picked the computer job. It was fun. But I think my life would have been just as interesting if I had taken the Tiffany job. Actually, it probably would have been even more surreal than it is now.

Q. *How were you introduced to cyberspace and what were your first experiences with it?*
A. I was first introduced to cyberspace in 1986 in grad school and I was an instant addict. All the people!

Q. *How did your online/new media career evolve?*
A. I started Echo in 1989 when I was in my last year of graduate school because I had nothing else to do and I had to think of something fast. (The company I was working for was moving to Virginia and I didn't want to go.) I thought turning my online addiction into a career was a particularly clever move on my part.

Q. *What is one of your most unusual online anecdotes?*
A. The adjective "unusual" is throwing me. Nothing is unusual to me about cyberspace, except how shockingly familiar it is compared to anywhere else.

Q. *What has been your most rewarding online or new media–related experience so far?*
A. We had a gang baby shower last month; because so many women on Echo were having babies at the same time, it was impossible to hold a separate shower for each of them. When I saw all the babies and the babies to come who would not be in this world were it not for Echo, I don't know what to say. I got all choked up, even though children scare me!

Q. *What are your favorite sites or online forums and why?*
A. I use the Internet Movie Database (http://www.imdb.com/) regularly because I am a movie fanatic and that site has everything you could possibly want to know about anything to do with movies. I also visit *Toshi's Web Journal* (http://www.itp.

tsoa.nyu.edu/~student/toshi/diary.html) often because he is the most charming writer on the Internet.

Q. *What advice would you give women regarding computers, the Internet, or technology in general?*
A. I can't think of a global piece of advice. I know! The pain of regret is far greater than the pain of failure, so do whatever it is you long to do.

Joan Korenman, Fifty-five

http://www.umbc.edu/wmst/

Q. *What is your official title and what do you do?*
A. My title is Professor of English and Director of Women's Studies. As the title suggests, I teach English and direct the Women's Studies Program at the University of Maryland, Baltimore County (UMBC).

Q. *What sites/forums/services are you responsible for creating—that is, what are the highlights of your career?*
A. Probably the thing I'm most proud of is starting WMST-L, an email list (i.e., forum) for women's studies teaching, research, and program administration, which I started in May 1991 and still run. The list now has over four thousand subscribers in forty-four countries.

I also created and maintain the UMBC Women's Studies website (http://www.umbc.edu/wmst/). When I started it in 1994, I was using a 286 computer with a 20 MB hard drive, so for the first two years I maintained the website with no Web access except through the text-based browser Lynx. It was, shall we say, a "graphics-challenged" site, and in many respects still is. Even so, it has received a good deal of acclaim, including being featured last year in a *U.S. News & World Report* cover story as one of the "best websites for women."

The two pages that get the most attention are Gender-Related Electronic Forums, an annotated, frequently updated listing of approximately three hundred women-related email lists, and Women's Studies/Women's Issues WWW Sites, a selective, frequently updated listing of information-rich websites that focus on women's studies/women's issues.

Q. *What is your educational background?*
A. I was trained to be an English professor, and that's what I am. I received a B.A. from Brandeis University and an M.A. and Ph.D. from Harvard, all in English and American literature. As I'm quick to point out, whenever I give talks or workshops on electronic communications, I have absolutely no technical background. I didn't even use a computer to write my dissertation—there were no PCs back then!

Q. *How were you first exposed to computers and what was your initial reaction to them?*
A. My husband was responsible for our buying an Apple II+ back in 1981. I spent a little time learning the fundamentals, but while I found it fun, I also regarded it as utterly irrelevant to the things I was then doing, so I let it go. In the mid-eighties, I started to use the computer a lot for word processing, and that was really the only use I made of it until I went online in 1990.

Q. *How were you introduced to cyberspace and what were your first experiences with it?*
A. My husband was an active email user in the 1980s, but I didn't have any interest until 1990, when a good friend at the University of Minnesota persuaded me to get an email account so we could communicate more easily. My friend also helped me find some email lists, and soon I was hooked! Indeed, by the spring of 1991, I started an email list of my own (WMST-L).

Q. *How did your online/new media career evolve?*
A. The hard part was trying to make my new passion for electronic communications fit somehow into my academic career. I was spending absurd amounts of time online, first with WMST-L and then also with the Women's Studies website. Fortunately, be-

cause I direct the Women's Studies Program, I soon found a connection, since most of my online activities focused on women's
studies. In fact, I began to see that my work online is actually a
logical extension of my other work in women's studies.

Those of us who work in women's studies must make sure
that women's experiences, accomplishments, and perspectives
are fully represented in the electronic world. If we do not,
there's a real danger that much of what women's studies has
achieved over the past thirty years will be lost, and women's experiences will once again be rendered invisible.

Q. *What is one of your most unusual online anecdotes?*
A. I'm not sure whether this is an unusual anecdote, but . . . I
started the WMST-L email list in the spring of 1991. Just a couple of days after I started WMST-L, I received an email message
from a New Zealand sociologist on sabbatical in Finland telling
me that he had learned of WMST-L from his colleagues in Finland, and that he had written to his colleagues back in New
Zealand to let them know about this valuable new resource.

I was blown away. WMST-L was only a few days old; none
of my colleagues in the English department at UMBC had the
slightest idea of its existence, and yet people already knew about
it in Finland and New Zealand. I'm not sure anyone else felt the
earth shrink that day, but I sure did!

Q. *What has been your most rewarding online or new media–related experience so far?*
A. What I've found most rewarding has been all the enthusiasm
and thanks that people have expressed to me about WMST-L.
They speak about WMST-L as being "absolutely invaluable"
and "a lifeline." It's a great feeling to know that I've been responsible for creating something that so many people value so
highly.

Q. *What are your favorite sites or online forums and why?*
A. I have many favorite websites; it's not possible to single out
just a few. With email forums, though, I have to confess that

WMST-L is my clear favorite. I love it because it keeps me informed about what's happening—events, trends, controversies, publications, films, research projects, classroom strategies and problems, new directions in women's studies, and so on.

I get exposed to debates and issues in fields outside my own. It's like having a group of very bright, interesting, articulate friends always there when I want them, but if I'm busy or in a funk, I can just ignore them without hurting their feelings. And now, when I go places, I continually meet people whom I "know" from the list.

Q. *What advice would you give women regarding computers, the Internet, or technology in general?*
A. Wow . . . It's hard to be concise here—I give whole talks and workshops on this topic. Also, it's hard to give advice to "women," since we're so varied. However, for those women who regard computers and the Internet apprehensively, I'd like to emphasize how much fun electronic communications can be. I would also urge people not to trust sensationalistic media accounts. All too often, newspapers, magazines, and television programs are more interested in attention grabbing than in presenting an accurate account.

I think it's vitally important that more women become involved with electronic communications. Increasingly, that's the channel through which all of us, women and men alike, will get our information. People without access to this technology, or who are afraid of it, will be like those in an earlier time (and even some today) who lacked access to books and literacy. A disproportionate number were/are women. I hope that, at least in a small way, I'm helping to change this.

Nancy Rhine, Forty-one

http://www.digitalcities.com/

Q. *What is your official title and what do you do?*
A. Director of Business Development for Digital City. I serve as somewhat of a talent scout—discovering and recruiting new and/or established talents, personalities, and businesses to deliver unique, and what I think will be highly popular, online programming. I'm also in charge of marketing and public relations as well as promotions.

Q. *What sites/forums/services are you responsible for creating—that is, what are the highlights of your career?*
A. I was on the management team at The WELL during its years of most rapid growth. I founded Women's Wire in 1992. I founded America Online's first women's area, Women's Network, in 1996. I'm currently one of the founders of Digital City San Francisco.

Q. *What is your educational background?*
A. I have a B.A. in liberal arts and postgraduate coursework in business.

Q. *How were you first exposed to computers and what was your initial reaction to them?*
A. I first got my hands on computers in 1982 when I put together a database for the first national midwives association in the United States. I was afraid if I hit the wrong key or did something wrong, the whole thing would crash. So I was very nervous.

Q. *How were you introduced to cyberspace and what were your first experiences with it?*
A. My longtime buddies founded The WELL in 1985, and so I was hearing all their management and community stories for a few years while they tried to convince me to get involved. In

1987, I joined as a user, and in 1989, they drafted me to come and work with them there.

I resisted using computers for anything other than what I perceived as making my life and my job easier in some concrete way. I was using computers as a professional bookkeeper while raising my three daughters as a single mom and had no time to get online—it didn't appear that it would make an important difference in my life, which was so crowded already.

It wasn't until I started working online full-time that I realized the power of this new medium, and I've been working online full-time as my career since then, which was May 1989.

Q. *How did your online/new media career evolve?*
A. I started doing customer support, then created organizational structure by designing departments, discovered I was good at management, strategizing, technical writing, communication, marketing, and PR. I discovered how much I loved business and communication, and discovered a much stronger entrepreneurial spirit than I realized I had.

I moved on to starting my own company, and then starting divisions for large corporations, as well as consulting for many companies along the way. Online management gave me a chance to marry my love for business and entrepreneuring with my love of interactive communication and people.

Q. *What has been your most rewarding online or new media–related experience so far?*
A. Oh, by far the ability to meet and stay in touch with so many fascinating people around the globe. I'd have to say that getting to train Gloria Steinem and getting to train the folks in the White House Women's Office were some of the most rewarding new media–related experiences I've had.

Q. *What are your favorite sites or online forums and why?*
A. My favorite sites and forums are always the ones I'm working on at the time. I don't have enough emotional bandwidth or time for more than one virtual community at a time, and I al-

ways like the one I'm working with at the time the most! So right now I love Digital City San Francisco!

Q. *What advice would you give women regarding computers, the Internet, or technology in general?*
A. Computers free us up to telecommute and start our own businesses to a much greater degree—very important in designing flexibility and empowerment into our work lives as women and more important, as mothers. I found this out as I designed my work environment and roles as a head of household and single mother.

So my advice would be for women to dive right in and become good at some aspect of online or computer technology that strikes their fancy—if you're not sure, take a few courses at the local community college or night school and see if any of the topics attract your attention and enthusiasm. Then keep going and you'll find yourself becoming more and more marketable! It truly is the Electronic Frontier and gender is not too much of a deterrent in this new territory.

Ellen Pack, Thirty-one

http://www.women.com/

Q. *What is your official title and what do you do?*
A. I am the Vice President of Product Development at Wire Networks, Inc. I manage the creative efforts for our network of websites, which includes editorial and design for three daily-changing websites. I also manage our content partnerships and content syndication. In addition, I head the creative team that develops new sites to add to our family of websites. We currently have two new sites under development.

Q. *What sites/forums/services are you responsible for creating—that is, what are the highlights of your career?*
A. I founded Wire Networks in 1992.

I have led the creative teams on Women's Wire (http://www.women.com), Beatrice's Web Guide (http://www.bguide.com), and *Prevention*'s Healthy Ideas (http://www.healthyideas.com). Of course, I had lots of help, particularly from our editor in chief, Laurie Kretchmar, and our art director, Lourdes Livingston.

I also authored a book/CD-ROM, *Women's Wire Web Directory* (Macmillan Computer Publishing, 1997).

Q. *What is your educational background?*
A. I received a B.A. from Columbia College in 1987. I received an M.B.A. from Columbia Business School in 1990.

Q. *How were you first exposed to computers and what was your initial reaction to them?*
A. I was first exposed to computers in high school when I took a computer programming class as an elective. I really liked it and took another programming class my freshman year in college. I knew I didn't want to be a programmer for a career, but the logic of computer programming appealed to me. I used computers throughout college and in all of my jobs since then.

Q. *How were you introduced to cyberspace and what were your first experiences with it?*
A. I introduced myself to cyberspace when I moved out to the Silicon Valley area from New York City. I got online for the first time to search for a place to live and learn more about the area. I was also using email for the software start-up where I was working. I was immediately enthralled with it and wanted to get all of my family members and friends online to make cross-country communications easier.

A few things really struck me about this new world: the lack of women online (about one in fifteen back in 1992), the paucity of interesting things to do online (what we now call content), and the amazing ability to meet and talk to people online I would have never otherwise met.

Q. *How did your online/new media career evolve?*
A. I was working for a start-up computer software company when I got the idea to start Women's Wire. I left the company I was working for to devote myself full-time to this effort in mid–1992 and I've been with Wire Networks ever since then.

My thought was if you build a service aimed at women's interests, more women would come online. And in fact women came on in droves. Today we make up over 40 percent of Internet users.

Q. *What is one of your most unusual online anecdotes?*
A. One of the things I love about the Internet is the spontaneity of communication and the way it bridges distances. One day I logged in and had an email waiting for me from an old boyfriend in France. He had tracked down my email address through one of the online directory services. I hadn't talked to him in ten years and it had been about that long since I tried to read a French letter, too. The last place I expected to hear from him was in email.

Q. *What has been your most rewarding online or new media–related experience so far?*
A. Everything I have had the opportunity to work on in new media has been rewarding because I like the mix of business, technology, and media. Getting a business off the ground, growing it, and raising capital have all been incredibly challenging. One of the things I enjoy most about my job is helping to create and shape websites that reach large and vocal audiences. Working with creative and talented people in a fast-paced, ever-changing medium really gets my adrenaline going.

Q. *What are your favorite sites or online forums and why?*
A. I have many favorite sites. I like Yahoo! (http://www.yahoo.com) because it puts the world at my fingertips. I like CNN (http://www.cnn.com) because I'm a news junkie. I go to Wired (http://www.wired.com) for industry news, and I like

Papermag (http://www.papermag.com) because it gives me a dose of New York when I get homesick.

Q. *What advice would you give women regarding computers, the Internet, or technology in general?*
A. I would advise women everywhere and at every age to get involved in computers, and the Internet for a million reasons. It will improve their access to information. It will broaden their world. It's a great career move. It's a way to stay in touch with more people inexpensively. It's more entertaining than television. And, if they get involved now, they can help create and shape this medium that is changing the way we communicate, live, and work.

Eva Shaderowfsky, Fifty-nine

http://www.webgrrls.com/eva/

Q. *What is your official title and what do you do?*
A. This has changed a lot over the six plus years I've been online. For more than a year, I was Online Coordinator for the new Women's Network on AOL.

Before that, there were a lot of other titles. Right now, and throughout the other titles I've held, I've been, in one form or another, the moderator for Evenings With Eva, a weekly, women's issues conference every Tuesday on AOL [9:00–10:30 P.M., ET. Keyword, EWE].

Q. *What sites/forums/services are you responsible for creating—that is, what are the highlights of your career?*
A. Evenings with Eva, conferences, founder/forum leader since September 1995; online coordinator, Women's Network, cofounder with Nancy Rhine; Women's Issues Conferences, IES, founder/forum leader from October 1994 through September 1995; CNN Women's Issues Conference, founder/moderator/host (June 1993 to October 1994); The Women's Room, founder/host (September 1991 to June 1995); consultant, moderator/host,

founder of Chat in Real Time (June 1994 to May 1995); Chronic Fatigue Support Group, founder/cohost (September 1992 to September 1993).

Q. *What is your educational background?*
A. B.A. Barnard College.

Q. *How were you first exposed to computers and what was your initial reaction to them?*
A. I have two grown sons. My younger son insisted I get a computer, since I'd been looking at them, talking about them, for years. A friend of his had an Apple IIc he was selling. I bought it and loved it.

Q. *How were you introduced to cyberspace and what were your first experiences with it?*
A. My elder son, after I got CFS [chronic fatigue syndrome], gave me a modem and the AOL software for my birthday. Miraculous, it seemed to me! First thing I did was to try to find a CFS support group. There wasn't one, so I started one.

Q. *How did your online/new media career evolve?*
A. Well, my résumé tells it in a way. :) It took a while to get the CFS support group going. I looked for a place to discuss women's issues. There were none.

So I started The Women's Room in People Connection on AOL. Then CNN asked me to do a women's issues conference for them. So I did. In the meantime, I spent a year as cohost in the Fiction Workshop, also on AOL. In addition, I spent a year as Lifestyles' suggestions coordinator . . . a fancy name, meaning that I answered suggestions in that area of AOL.

After that, and while I was still running The Women's Room and the CNN Women's Issues Conference, you [Aliza] suggested that I take a look at Women's Wire. I did, and since I can't be passive, I started Chat in Real Time there, a weekly women's issue chat, which I ran for a year or so. That's where I met Nancy Rhine, cofounder of Women's Wire.

When Nancy became director of women's programming for AOL, she asked me to work with her to create and run the area that's now known as the Women's Network. By the way, the CNN Women's Issues Conference is now in the Women's Network and is known as Evenings With Eva . . . Nancy suggested the name change.

Q. *What is one of your most unusual online anecdotes?*
A. When I first signed on, I was a regular in the Writers Den, a weekly review of writings by wannabes, held in People Connection on AOL. There was a man there whose comments were extremely insightful. Since his screen name suggested the air force, I imagined he was a retired, very intelligent man, somewhere in his fifties.

We spent a lot of time sending Instant Messages to each other . . . a form of private communication . . . about the work being discussed. He asked if he could talk some more, and whether I'd meet him in a private room online. Since he hadn't come on to me, I thought this was a fine idea and we could talk as much as we wanted. We set up a time. That day, I worried a bit. Were his motives as clean as they seemed? What if I was wrong about his age? Would he be reluctant to talk with a woman in her fifties?

So, came the meeting time, with me nervous about the whole thing. First thing I said to him was something like, "We haven't mentioned age . . ." Before I could type another word, he said, "Age? Oh, yes. Well, I'll tell you. I'm 16 and a half." LOL!!! So much for this unseen environment where prejudices about age, etcetera, don't come into play. I love it. It's the great leveler.:)

Q. *What has been your most rewarding online or new media–related experience so far?*
A. Hard to say which has been most rewarding for me. I loved creating the content and acting as administrator for the Women's Network. Working with Nancy Rhine and being responsible to 150+ remote staffers was a tremendous amount of work. But it was vital to me and like a dream come true.

Q. *What are your favorite sites or online forums and why?*

A. I don't usually have time to do a lot of surfing around—except when it's work-related. I love all of Aliza's creations [AUTHOR'S NOTE: I didn't pay her to say this!], as well as FAIR (http://www.igc.org/fair/), Electric Minds (http://www.minds.com), and I do visit Women's Access (http://www.grfxsoup.com/sonya/guide.htm) for resources. It's a wonderful place, like finding a bookstore with just what you'd like to read. And, I have to add, I like my own forum quite a bit (Evenings With Eva).

Q. *What advice would you give women regarding computers, the Internet, or technology in general?*

A. I'd say—and I do say—to every woman: Get online! If you need help, find someone. To friends and acquaintances I say, If I can help, ask me. You *need* to be online. To not be online is a bit like not having a telephone. Imagine how daunting that was when it first came out, and now everyone has one. This technology is moving quickly and you'll be left behind if you don't take part in it. Sooner or later you'll have to anyway. So why not now? Do it!:)

The truth is that I find men more reluctant to get online the first time than women. Their excuses are not along the lines of the technology being daunting. They say they've lived without this for so long and done fine. Therefore, no need for it. Or they say it's another passive time-waster. Ha!

Susan Defife, Thirty-five

http://www.womenconnect.com

Q. *What is your official title?*

A. President and CEO, Women's Connection Online.

Q. *What sites/forums/services are you responsible for creating—that is, what are the highlights of your career?*

A. Founded Women's Connection Online, a thoughtful, intelligent community for women on the Internet. Aimed at professional women and women business owners, WCO offers daily news of interest to women; resource channels such as business/career, politics, health, finance, and so on; a regional events calendar; listing of women's organizations, links to related women's sites on the Internet, and discussion groups.

Q. *What is your educational background?*
A. Two years of college (University of Delaware).

Q. *How were you first exposed to computers and what was your initial reaction to them?*
A. Eighteen years ago, never having used a computer, I signed up for a computer science class at my university. One class period of COBOL discussions later, my head spinning, I withdrew. I didn't touch a computer for five years.

For ten years, I excelled at word processing! Even learned an internal email system that I used for a couple of years. Did not want to touch spreadsheets, databases, and such. With that one computer science class etched in my brain, my perception was it was too difficult.

Q. *How were you introduced to cyberspace and what were your first experiences with it?*
A. Three years ago, while consulting with women's organizations on strategic communications issues, I was contacted by a group of individuals who were putting together a company to develop an online network for a large consumer organization. I told them I was happy to help, but I would need a crash course in what they were talking about. My only information about cyberspace was obtained through television ads for Prodigy, which at that point was one of the first entrants in the online access race.

Midway through the company's presentation about the Internet, I realized this was an incredibly powerful tool that women needed. It provided the opportunity to disseminate valuable information in a time-efficient and cost-effective manner and to develop a cohesive global community by enabling women to communicate with one another, network, and build relationships.

I began to explore the Internet and various online services, asked women why they weren't online (at the time, only 10 percent of the online population was female) and what they were looking for in an online experience. As a "nontechie," I empathized with their frustration in using the Internet—too graphic-intensive (therefore too time-intensive), too much "noise" making it difficult to determine the junk from the "good stuff," no relevant material for women, an atmosphere that did not take women seriously, and few opportunities to build relationships with other women who shared similar concerns.

Using the information we gathered, we created an online community—initially, a private, subscriber-based service—providing information that is both purposeful and relevant, opportunities to discuss issues with other women, and easy navigation. Following an overwhelming response from our members, we converted to an Internet site last year to provide more women access to our community.

Q. *How did your online/new media career evolve?*
A. My background is very diverse; seemingly no connection to the positions I've held. But my experiences came together very nicely in the founding of my company, Women's Connection Online, Inc.

I have worked in television and radio as a reporter, editor, broadcaster, and talk-show host. I also did a stint in government as assistant press secretary to a governor, and then served as executive director of a nonprofit, nonpartisan women's organization, Women Executives in State Government. After WESG, I started my own public relations/communications firm.

Q. *What has been your most rewarding online or new media–related experience so far?*
A. Seeing the rapid increase in the number of women online (from 10 percent when I started my company to 42 percent today) and hearing the reactions to what we're providing for

women: "What a great resource," "Wow! I almost gave up on the Internet before I found your site," "There's nothing out there like this."

We respected the intelligence and time constraints of women and recognized their desire to find useful information and to be part of a community where they can build relationships with others. I'd like to think that the work we and the other women pioneers in cyberspace are doing is the key reason why women are coming online in such great numbers—they understand the power of the Internet and now have resources that make their online experience worthwhile.

Q. *What are your favorite sites or online forums and why?*
A. GolfWeb (http://www.golfweb.com)—Not a golfer, but a fan of well-done online communities, I admire the value this site imparts to its community with rich, useful content, interactive tools, tips, polls, discussion groups, and valuable products and premium member services.

Quicken Financial Network (http://www.qfn.com)—Valuable content; interaction tools for retirement planning and debt reduction; access to stock and mutual fund quotes; rates on personal loans, credit cards, and savings accounts; and insurance quotes.

Allpolitics (http://allpolitics.com)—Comprehensive information leading up to election day with detailed analysis of races and great real-time election results.

Q. *What advice would you give women regarding computers, the Internet, or technology in general?*
A. This is the future. If we don't take advantage of this technology now, we will once again be left behind.

Stephanie Brail, Twenty-seven

http://www.amazoncity.com/

Q. *What is your official title and what do you do?*
A. Stephanie Brail, President and Founder of Digital Amazon, a web development company for women.

Digital Amazon creates online content and communities for women. We also provide Internet consulting and Web development primarily for women-owned businesses and organizations. Our main project is Amazon City: the first city for women on the Internet at http://www.amazoncity.com.

Q. *What sites/forums/services are you responsible for creating—that is, what are the highlights of your career?*
A. Creating Amazon City, an award-winning online community and resource center for women. We offer discussion forums in our Amazon City Cafe, Amazon City Radio, netcasting to women on the Internet, original content, resources, and more.

Founding Spiderwoman, the original mailing list for women Web designers. Founded in 1995, Spiderwoman started out as an Internet mailing list, and has since expanded to include a Web conferencing system and a sister list for women in the online business world, SpiderwomanBiz. Spiderwoman is organizing a women's summit to discuss the future of technology, in response to Bill Gates's mostly male CEO Summit.

I wrote a chapter on online sexual harassment and free speech for *Wired Women: Gender and New Realities and Cyberspace* (Seal Press).

Q. *What is your educational background?*
A. I have a B.A. in English and music from the University of Michigan, Ann Arbor.

I was initially in the engineering program but quit because I did not like the dehumanized way the curriculum was set up. A switch into computer science did not last too long, when I found that my teachers seemed more interested in "weeding people out" than teaching. I found the humanities programs to be much more focused on actually teaching, and the professors, as a whole, were much more accessible and helpful in these programs as opposed to the technical programs.

Q. *How were you first exposed to computers and what was your initial reaction to them?*
A. My dad started getting into PCs as a hobby when I was a kid, about ten years old. I loved computers! I used to stay up all night playing computer games. Eventually, Dad bought me my own computer (an 8088!) when I was sixteen. My dad always told me I'd need to know computers to have a job someday, and I credit him with my success.

Q. *How were you introduced to cyberspace and what were your first experiences with it?*
A. Once again, it was my dad who got me online. When I went to college he purchased a Prodigy account so we could keep in touch via email. I used to read the Prodigy horoscopes to my roommates in college. Soon I got my free university email account (U of M was an excellent school when it came to computers) and started getting my feet wet on the Internet. This was 1988.

Q. *How did your online/new media career evolve?*
A. I used to be a freelance writer, and started using the Internet to research my articles and interview people. Then someone sent me an email about some Internet classes that the person was selling. I decided it might be fun to teach as a way to make some extra money. I contacted this person about teaching the courses and soon I was the main instructor (part-time) for the Los Angeles Internet Group. As a teacher, I had many people coming up to me after class asking for consulting help or wanting me to make a website for them (this was in 1994), so I started my own Web consulting business.

I soon found I was really the only woman I knew doing Internet consulting in Los Angeles. I founded Digital Amazon in

1995 with a friend (who is no longer in the business) as a way to support women in technology. I also started the Spiderwoman mailing list simply because I wanted to know there were other women out there doing what I was doing. I was happy to find out there were a lot of great women in the field!

Now, after spending years developing websites for clients, I am focusing on creating and publishing my own content. There are certain needs I see that have to be fulfilled and I want to be a part of creating quality space for women online that goes beyond just the traditional makeup and fashion magazines.

Q. *What is one of your most unusual online anecdotes?*
A. My big fifteen minutes of fame was an experience of online harassment I had in 1993—it also inspired me to start a business to support women. The story is in the book *Wired Women*.

Q. *What has been your most rewarding online or new media–related experience so far?*
A. Seeing the community that formed in Spiderwoman and in the Amazon City Cafe. It's nice to create something that goes beyond yourself and becomes something greater. I love to see how people have created friendships and supported one another with these forums.

Q. *What are your favorite sites or online forums and why?*
A. Personally, I enjoy sites that offer community interaction. I have always been a regular on The WELL, but have been less active in the last year. Only recently have I started to join more online forums. My current favorite, besides our own Amazon City Cafe Web conferencing system, which I am quite addicted to personally, is Electric Minds (http://www.minds.com). It's free and offers a great interface with intelligent conversation.

I also enjoy Tripod (http://www.tripod.com), since it offers a slightly quirky magazine/community for people my age. I also belong to various mailing lists for women. I also enjoy quality news sites such as CNET (http://www.news.com) and *The Wall Street Journal* Interactive (http://www.wsj.com).

Q. *What advice would you give women regarding computers, the Internet, or technology in general?*

A. Just jump into it and don't be afraid that you'll break your computer!

Start your own business—we need more women leaders and we need to create our own support systems. We need to reshape technology to make it more women-friendly and people-sensitive. Only by taking the lead can we really effect positive change.

Chapter 14   Mothers and Grandmothers

The Web has a wealth of resources and communities for mothers and parents in general, but even more interesting are the sites created by moms themselves who have taken it upon themselves to use the Web to fill a need they've seen.

From Kim Foglia's Working Moms' Internet Refuge (http://www.moms-refuge.com), which provides resources to busy moms, to Sue Anne Kendall (http://www.prairienet. org/~sak), who has resources about breastfeeding and La Leche groups (http://www.lalecheleague.org/), to Cindy Johns, who has a website about homeschooling (http://www.kaleidoscapes. com/), moms are helping other moms by providing them with essential tools for parenting that are accessible any time of the day or night.

```
From: Cindy Johns

From my own experience I've found that for
women (particularly those of us who are moms),
knowledge, growth, and the Internet all entwine
together like a beautifully plaited braid.
Intellectual growth is based on the desire to
undertake new challenges, and because of that
desire.

Kaleidoscapes gave rise to the first independent
Web-based homeschool forum in 1995; and I am
exceptionally proud of that accomplishment. I
encourage other women to make the effort to learn
the basics for joining the online world and do
some growing of their own. It's getting easier
every day.

For me, like many moms, one of the most important
goals in life is to see that kids get a quality
education; and merging the Internet with education
```

is ideal. The Internet offers them the freedom to
develop as individuals, and not be corralled into
a "cookie-cutter" mold. The homeschool community
is enjoying explosive growth all over the world,
and with the use of Internet bulletin boards we're
able to share successful techniques and resources
to instill an enthusiastic joy for learning in our
kids' hearts.

My most rewarding experiences, with regards to
the Internet, are the times when I see fellow
homeschooling parents getting through tough
situations by using the discussion boards to
communicate their problems and fears to others who
have "been there and done that." It's an awesome
feeling to realize that with these discussion
boards, I'm helping an entire community to grow
and evolve; and as a woman, I love having the
opportunity to learn and develop my own Web skills
while I take my kids, the Kaleidoscapes website,
and fellow home educators to greater heights using
the Internet.

One of my favorite stories about moms online is how women
who are pregnant and due a certain month can join a forum or
an Internet mailing list with other women due at the same time.
They can go through each month of their pregnancy knowing they have an entire network of other women going through
the exact same physical and emotional changes they are going
through.

For women who might not have any friends or relatives
nearby who have recently been or are currently pregnant, the
Internet brings them to a warm community of women who can
relate to their experiences, give them feedback and advice, or
just be available to "listen" at a moment's notice.

If you are pregnant, here's how to subscribe to one of those lists: Send email to listserv@lists.csi.net, and in the body of your message type:

```
subscribe [MONTH]
```

(Insert your due month, but don't include the brackets—for example: subscribe july)

If you ever want to remove yourself from this mailing list, you can send email to listserv@lists.csi.net with the following command in the body of your email message:

```
unsubscribe [MONTH NAME] [EMAILADDRESS]
```

Another good resource for women who are going through pregnancy (and for the men in their lives as well): many moms-to-be recommend the Usenet Newsgroup: misc.kids.pregnancy.

But what about earlier generations of women, women who have never been exposed to computers in school or in the workplace? There are thousands of mature women online who have not let fear of the unknown stop them from getting online and definitely did not let age become a barrier or excuse for not getting connected to the Internet.

```
From: Almita Ranstrom,
http://www.vashonisland.com/almitasgallery

I call myself the cybergrannie (old and wired).
I have been an artist all my life (a long time),
did all the ArtPolitik, taught art at Cal State
Fullerton, etc. and eventually realized that older
women cannot go far in that world. The unexpected
arrival of resident grandchildren and loss of my
part-time teaching job drove me to learning
digital "fine" art, where my studio is my desktop.

After my husband retired and we moved to Vashon
Island, Washington, I discovered the World Wide
```

Web and recognized that in this arena I could do as I pleased. So I learned enough HTML to design and create my own little gallery, traded some design work for a place on our local home pages, did it all without agents, government grants, or a lot of encouragement.

After joining Seattle Webgrrls [see "Cybergrrl Resources on the Web"], I managed to start getting some exposure, made a lot of new friends, did the same with a couple of other lists, and feel that I have more positive feedback than I ever had before. This has changed my life. Now I have a place to show art, people to see it, and a feeling that I am in charge of it all. I don't sell work; all the current work is in digital form only, and I can get away with being a cranky old lady! What freedom!

Pat Hughes, sixty-one, has a thirty-year-old daughter who shares her AOL membership when she visits. As a writer, she has found a world of support and information on America Online and the Internet. "They're not just information bases, they're communities, especially the women's area," explains Pat. "I'm not a technophobe, but I'm certainly not any threat to Bill Gates, and lots of my experience with computers has been online. It feeds my need to discover and explore without actually having to rappel up the sides of cliffs or risk my hide. And, of course, there are writers' connections. I've met some older gentlemen in the pen pals and love connection areas, and we've had cyber-friendships that have been interesting."

Other examples of mature women using the Net are in the profiles given in Chapter 13. Both Eva Shaderowfsky and Joan Korenman are women over fifty who do not come from techni-cal backgrounds, which goes to show that it's not just the younger "digital age" women who are going online.

Chapter 15   Writers and Artists

The Web is a powerful publishing tool that is much more accessible to women than the traditional publishing routes. Lesa Whyte explains: "The Web changed my life by being a new medium to express myself. I have always considered myself a writer/artist, but I was unhappy with the current modes of expression available to me. The Web allowed me to explore my creativity and to allow other people to participate in my vision."

Through her independent electronic 'zine, *The Redrum Coffeehouse* (http://www.gothitica.com/redrum/), she began publishing art in the horror/gothic genre. She has a subscriber base of about 150 people, which, she says, "is enough to give me a reason to pursue this creative project." She solicits art from other writers, poets, artists, and humorists around the world through the Web and has even made friends as a result of publishing online.

From: Sandra Kinsler

I'd always wanted to be in the publishing business
and never had the opportunity to participate. The
Web provided that opportunity. At the beginning of
1996, with no financial support, my husband, Brian
Leshon, and I started an Internet magazine called
Woman Motorist. It is an automotive magazine for
women (and men) on the Web. We felt that there was
a wide-open market for car-related information
structured specifically for women and men for whom
no particular level of expertise or knowledge was
assumed. We had watched a print-based automotive
magazine for women struggle to receive shelf
space. The Web has very few barriers to entry,
although some misogyny and skepticism about the
effectiveness of women's work efforts still exist.
Despite that, we have over 100,000 monthly readers

and obtain all of our revenue from advertising
sales. We've been able to do what we were told
could not be done: provide women with quality
automotive information, motivate them to read it,
and make a living at it. We plan to roll out
several more women's market niche publications
over the next couple of years.

Karen Peeters from Brussels, Belgium, calls herself a "creative person." She's an art teacher, a hat designer, and a "decoratrice" (she specializes in Christmas decorations). When she began designing her first hat collection, she used the Web to let the media know what she was doing.

Since then she has created her own website where she shows her hat designs (http://www.club.innet.be/~ind1028). She has met other hat designers through the Web from other countries to talk about the technical aspects of hat design.

Xander Mellish runs a site for short stories and cartoons (http://www.xmel.com/). Before the World Wide Web existed, she used to post her short stories on telephone poles and in pizza parlors and Laundromats around the city. "I was just looking for an audience," Xander explains. "I knew my stories were good, but I had no connections, I was a nobody, and my style wasn't a particularly fashionable one. I wasn't part of the whole clique that had evolved around creative writing degree programs, which I hate. I was writing wonderful stories, but I had no way of being read."

The Web changed all that for Xander. Suddenly, she was in charge of the publishing process.

From: Xander

I could present my stories the way I wanted,
without financial backing from a publishing house.
I didn't have to wait two years for my work to
go from manuscript to proof to sales sample to
bookstore product. The stories could be read as

quickly as I wrote them. What's more, I got direct
response from readers, who made it very clear
which stories they liked and which ones they
didn't.

I was also able to stretch the boundaries of
what was called a book, by including audio clips,
reader comments, and a changing gallery of
drawings and photographs relating to the stories.

The Internet is the future of American fiction.
In book form, American literature is controlled
by a small circle of people. But on the Internet,
writers are in charge. They control the
presentation and distribution of their own work.

For some writers—namely the ones who can't
write!—this may be a disastrous event. But
for everyone else, the Internet is the best
development for writers since Gutenberg. We
can have mass readership without being backed
by mass capital. A lot of new voices are going
to be heard.

Jeanna Gollihur had been talking about a new career for ten
years but didn't know what to do. Her skills included painting
houses, taping Sheetrock, and setting tile—work she did to support herself and her son—as well as songwriting and performing.
"I used a word processor to take a correspondence course in
writing, but kept on doing the labor," she explained.

After moving into a community house that had a computer,
the possibility of using email convinced her to get online so she
could communicate with her family. She then heard about a
woman publisher, and she wrote to her about her desire to write.
Jeanna sent a poem via email and the publisher suggested she
create an animated graphic for the Web to depict the poem. "I,
of course, had no idea what this was, but for some reason I knew
I could do it," says Jeanna.

She talked to all her friends and went online to participate in chatrooms, learning about the programs she needed to use and the places online where she could download the software. She learned HTML (the programming "language" for building websites) from tutorials, designed her own personal website (http://www.baileygrp.com/life), and put her "cyberpoems" online.

From: Sherry Miller,
http://www.sherryart.com/sherry/current.html

Lately I've been describing myself as the Oldest Woman on the Web (http://www.sherryart.com/sherry/columns/oldest.html). I moved from Maine to California in late 1991 with a Mac 512K for word processing. Less than 6 months later I was into and writing about multimedia, and by the end of 1992, I was publishing magazines online.

How did I learn these things? I was driven by the ability to publish instantly, to publish without editors removing humor from articles, to publish without overhead or costs, and to receive instant feedback from any article. When the Web came along, it was a natural medium for writers and artists.

I created my own award-winning website, SherryArt, in July 1995 and have been a very successful Web consultant since then. "SherryArt—where art and technology meet, and when they don't, humor steps in to do the job" has been my passion for 2 years. When I have too many clients, I neglect my site. It has 10 sections, 9 of which are displayed in a quilt format.

My artist son tells me I have it all—quilts, feminism, technology. I also publish my own columns and my own artwork. There is a picture of

me naked wrapped in an American flag. I love the
uncensored Web.

Although I don't see it this way, the Internet
affected my life by providing a totally new
unimagined career. That's how it looks to
outsiders. For me, the Internet is a new tool or
medium for the expression of creativity. Even
before the Web was available, I would say that if
you put a painting up on the Internet, more people
will be able to see it in one week than have seen
a Rembrandt in 400 years.

People rarely understand that an artist's work is
to express a vision of life. In expressing our
visions, hopefully we allow a deep connection to
happen between ourselves and other people. We are
expressing the relationship between all humans.
To do this, artists in every medium use the tools
that are available.

For me, the Internet and multimedia (sound,
animation, graphics) are a whole new set of tools
for expressing my vision. My life is moving
along—always an artist and a writer but now in a
new medium.

Chapter 16   Women Making Connections

Social

Kathryn Koromilas (http://www.geocities.com/Athens/ Acropolis/1969/room.htm and http://www.zip.com.au/~kk/ echo.htm), a teacher of English as a second language to adults, initially began using the Internet for social chatting to meet people from all over the world who shared her interests in philosophy and education.

She also created her own website with poetry and even a list of her favorite books, including *The Alchemist* by Paolo Coelho. She recounts how Mr. Coelho actually emailed her to thank her for mentioning his book on her personal website. "He told me that I had misspelled his name. Then he invited me to link to his own website." Which she did.

Margie Wilhelm had gone to school in the Philippines, on an air force base, which made it difficult for her to be in touch with former schoolmates. An alumnus from her high school (Wagner High School, Clark Air Force Base) put up a website (http://www.whoa.org) and started an Internet mailing list with incredible results. Alumni from the early sixties to the early nineties have all joined the mailing list. "We have exchanged terrific memories and reforged old friendships," Margie says.

Family

From: Caroline Blecherman, fifty-eight, educator

The Net has been an irreplaceable resource for keeping in touch with my scattered, yet close family. I'm in Connecticut and my daughter is in San Francisco, and we planned her wedding via email! Two years ago, when my son separated from his wife (he also lives in California), the entire family support system was available to him night

and day because of email! (That's a whole book
unto itself!)

My sister, with whom I am very, very close, lives
in south Florida and we can write each other 3
or 4 times a day when we need to, and when our
mother was dying, we needed to! For the past year,
our entire family (descendants of my grandfather)
have been planning our first-ever Family Reunion.
Without the Net, it would have been completely
impossible—but we are all getting together in
Gatlinburg, Tennessee, in 2 months!

Yes, this has profoundly changed not only my life
but the life of my entire family—all for the
better.

Kathleen Lange (http://weber.u.washington.edu/~klange), a
pediatric nurse practitioner, created and maintains a website for
her father's real estate business, which, she says, "has given us
something in common and strengthened our relationship."

Christine Kossman (http://www.i2.i-2000.com/~ckossman),
a forty-seven-year-old housewife "armed with just a high school
education," as she describes herself, went online before there
were graphical Web browsers and was "hooked."

When personal websites became popular, she decided to
create one as a birthday present for her son, who is gay. "I
learned HTML and put up a webpage in his honor," explains
Christine. "Since then, my page has been featured on MSN [the
Microsoft Network] and *Netguide* magazine, and will be in a new
book titled *Gay and Lesbian Resources on the Internet*." Christine
receives hundreds of emails from parents and gay teens asking
for help.

Daniela Cerrato lives in New York City, having moved to
the United States just a few years ago. "Phone bills were keeping
me from a good communication with my family," says Daniela.
"As soon as I got my own email account, our long-distance relationship changed radically." Now Daniela has what she calls "a

daily triangle communication" using email between her mother in Milan and brother in London. "My mother tells everybody 'Thanx to the email, I can stay away from my kids without suffering!' "

Lisa Sulgit has taken family communication a step further by registering her family name with the Internic (to reserve her website address) in order to create a website for her family reunion in the summer.

Romantic

When her boyfriend was in Australia, Charley Buntrock (http://pubweb.nwu.edu/~cjb168) attempted to save money by using various chat services online on a daily basis. "It was a lifesaver to our relationship, as well as our wallets," says Charley.

She confesses that she usually stays away from the "traditional chatrooms." Having a name like "Charley" has provided "interesting" encounters, such as the time when she was playing online backgammon and was mistakenly approached by women who thought she was a man.

Jane Bynum (http://www.grafika.com), a graphic designer, uses the Web to showcase her children's illustrations. She also met her husband online two and a half years ago and they were married a year ago.

From: Jane Bynum

The REAL story is that my husband had an ad online whereby he was looking to make friends via the Internet. (This was November 1994.) He was tired of meeting "younger" women on the campus where he was working on his Ph.D. (He was about 6 to 8 years older than most of them.) And I was frustrated with the limited pool of intelligent, liberal men in the conservative Midwest town where I was living with my then 8-year-old son.

So . . . I went "surfin" on the Net. Actually, I met several nice people on Prodigy (that was the service we both used then). Had some interesting email discussions with many. Had to weed out some real weirdos, too. But, overall, cyberdating was quite fun and enlightening.

I responded to Paul's ad and we maintained a 6-week correspondence before meeting. We got to know a lot about each other via those emails— enough to know that we were interested in meeting face-to-face. He lived about 150 miles away in a larger city. And, as fate would have it, he had received his master's degree from the university in my Midwest town of 100,000. So he knew the area. We rendezvoused at a local restaurant/bar near campus, decided we had interest in pursuing the relationship, went out again that night, then didn't meet again for a couple of weeks.

I cannot say that either of us had a "love-at-first-sight" reaction. We both found the other attractive and (admittedly) were relieved that neither had horns growing out of our heads (or some other strange anomaly)—but the transition from cyberdating to REAL dating was just that: a transition. Somewhere along the way we fell in love. On weekends when my son was with his father, Paul and I visited each other's homes, traveling by train or car. It was quite romantic at this point. We dated (in person) for over a year and were married in March 1996.

We found in each other wonderful support, love, and respect. Although we come from two cultures (he is Nigerian and I am American Caucasian), we find that our greatest challenges are simply

managing our intense personalities. The culture
differences are real and sometimes more apparent
than we would like for them to be. But, for the
most part, the culture differences are minor. His
family is wonderful (I met them in Nigeria last
summer) and my parents and son love him dearly.

When people ask how we met, I love to watch their
reaction when we say "on the Internet." It is such
a foreign concept to most. But as more and more
people use the Internet to satisfy business and
personal needs, I think we will see more and more
cybercouples like us.

Michelle Boudreault was a chemical engineering student at
the University of Alberta, Canada, who met her boyfriend online. "I was living in Edmonton, Alberta, and he was living in
Toronto, Ontario," she recounts. They began talking about their
respective lives. Eventually, she moved to Toronto to live with
him, they've started their own business and they've had a baby
together.

From: Michelle

We met on IRC when we were both in the middle of
divorces. We became good friends and shoulders for
each other to cry on. We started to communicate
via email and on the phone as well as on IRC.

We met each other in person when I took a vacation
trip (brain-break as I like to call it) to Toronto
and Montreal. I had decided to take the trip so
that I could meet in real life (IRL) all the
interesting people I'd met online.

I met Marc about halfway through my trip at a
get-together that had been planned for me at
his (then) cybercafe. It was very interesting

because up until that point we had only been good
friends and confidants. I'm sure you can guess the
rest . . . the chemistry etc.

He had set aside that Tuesday specifically for us
to get to know each other IRL as well as we did
online. Well . . . one day turned into two, and
then into 4 before he accompanied me to Montreal,
where we continued my vacation (a few days behind
schedule;-) together. I went home a couple of days
later and the relationship continued via email,
IRC, and telephone. Let me say that I think we
helped Bell Canada advance its technology
significantly with the size of our bills.;-)

After that, we decided that I would move to
Toronto so that we could be together. Between the
vacation and the move, he flew to see me twice and
I to see him once more.

It was not long after I moved here that our
daughter (Calla) was conceived. She's the light
of both of our lives!:-)

Amy Zisman Gold was reading through the postings on
the "alt.personals.jewish" newsgroup one day, when she saw an
ad that looked interesting "because the guy posting seemed so
normal."

From: Amy

I debated for a couple of days and then finally
decided to reply to him directly using his email
address. He replied within the hour, which sort
of frightened me, but I gave him the benefit of
the doubt and we exchanged email for a couple
of weeks. Soon we exchanged phone numbers and then
met for iced tea. Seventeen months after our first

email contact we were married. Replying to his posting was one of the best decisions I have ever made!

Jessica Adelson sent me her romantic Internet story via email just seventy-two hours before her wedding day.

From: Jessica

Jeff and I have been together for six years. Our proposal is very special to me, because the way Jeff proposed really reflects his ability to know me, and how to reach me. He is incredibly perceptive.

One Saturday before Christmas Day, and after a fun morning filled with shopping, Jeff lured me to the local cybercafe. He said he was going to show me a Web page he built for his Notre Dame alumni friends before the big Fiesta Bowl. This was the winter of 1995, and as webmaster for *NetGuide* magazine's website, I was very involved in everything Internet.

Jeff, as a banker, knew close to nothing about the Internet, except for the fact that this crazy technology absorbed almost all of my time and energy, and my conversation (which, as my friends know, can be nonstop).

Once at the cafe, we pulled up a seat next to a computer, and I immediately took control of the mouse (as I tend to do) and started pointing and clicking my way through my favorite sites. Jeff finally asked me to give him an honest critique of his first Web attempt.

To build the site, he had signed up with America Online, and used its personal home page builder.

When that didn't work, he grabbed a copy of InContext software off my bookshelf and used it. He worked on the site late at night in his office, scanning pictures, coding links . . . the whole nine yards.

So I skeptically typed in his URL and waited for the first page to load. It was a picture of his old dorm mates, lined up outside his college dorm. The links were to the college home page, the sister college home page, other inside jokes for his friends. I needed no prodding to explore the page further and evaluate Jeff's html technique.

The last link on the page was to "Who's dating Who . . . What's the Latest Gossip." I click and link and wait as a page loads slowly. The picture is of Jeff in a suit, kneeling down and holding a ring outstretched in front of him. I stare at it puzzled, wondering, "Why is his picture there? Why is he kneeling?" Believe me, I had no clue.

Then the text popped up and stated "My dearest Jessica, will you marry me?" I am sure the Internet surfers sitting in the cafe had NO IDEA what was going on, and I am not sure I did really, as I had an out-of-body type of experience. When I turned to face him across the table, in front of me was a beautiful ring, and the impact of the moment had me in shock. Needless to say, my answer to his creative and sensitive proposal was yes!—I sent my answer to him via email :-)

Chapter 17   Wired Businesswomen

Chris Foster, a calligrapher and designer for over twenty years with her own business, moved to a rural area and felt isolated. She discovered Cyberscribes, an online group of "Calligraphers, Lettering Artists and Letter Lovers" from all over the world. With over 450 members, the group turned out to be a "tremendous source for information on tools, techniques, events and most of all camaraderie!" Chris receives sixty to seventy email posts each day from the list. "Discussions are ongoing. All questions are answered immediately. We even have a study group that uses the site to upload our homework for everyone's viewing and critiques. What a powerful group!" Chris exclaims.

"The Net has allowed me to remain in contact with partners in creative ventures and in business ventures (sometimes the two are the same)," says Molly Gordon (http://www.halcyon.com/molly), an artist, PR person, and coach. In addition to allowing multimedia collaborations online and access to technical support for her art and computer work, the Internet has been a means of promoting her coaching business. Says Molly, "My most satisfying coaching job began when my client found my Web page" on an international page about coaching.

From: Alison Berke, Web designer
http://www.bworks.com/

The Internet has become so much a part of my daily
life that I cannot imagine how I was able to keep
my communications and business running without
it. It would be like trying to manage without a
telephone, a newspaper, or reference books.

Business matters no longer depend on "telephone
tag" (leaving messages back and forth, without
being able to go into detail about the purpose of
my call). If I need information for a contract,
transaction, or meeting, I can send an immediate

email (in complete detail), and probably get an answer back (also in complete detail) sooner than waiting for a phone call that I may not be able to take because I am on the line with another customer.

Besides correspondence, it has become an information retriever for me. I track news, stocks, and even weather. I use the Internet to make travel arrangements (both business and personal), to gather information for particular projects I'm working on (e.g., to study a particular market or find reference information about different businesses), to locate lost articles from different magazines and newspapers, and to find contact information on a particular company or news story that I had seen on television or read about in print. I've even done research for speeches that I've written, as well as used the Internet for fact verification.

And I cannot even begin to explain how important the Webgrrls networking group [see "Cybergrrl Resources on the Web"] has been to my success as a business owner. In about five minutes, I learned the importance of the Internet and its technology through interacting with Webgrrls listserves and websites, and developing connections worldwide, which would have been impossible any other way than through the Internet.

There is so much information available now on the Internet that if you want to succeed in business, you MUST know how to use this technology.

I've seen the Internet (and all this new media technology) as the "new frontier" for business. And the way I see it, women finally have the opportunity to be 50/50 on a par with men who also

have to learn this new technology quickly. We
have the opportunity to break ground on the same
playing field as men, and get out of the starting
gate at the exact same time (too many metaphors?).

Ruby Yeh founded a "virtual company" consisting mostly of
women, all of whom work from their homes. She says, "The
Net has enabled me to create the type of business I've always
dreamed of working for, where there is no hierarchy and everyone is able to maintain her own entrepreneurial independence.
And the business is an online community where people have the
opportunity to share and learn about how the Net can be used to
improve their lives and even enable them to 'reach for their
dreams.' "

From: Ruby Yeh, http://folksonline.com/

The key point which I'd like to share is that the
Internet is the most valuable tool available for
anyone to pursue her professional and personal
goals, regardless of gender, race, or any other
characteristics. Without the usual physical
interaction, which generates the standard
prejudices, each individual's contribution on the
Net is experienced by other parties in a more pure
form because their preconditioned beliefs are not
triggered.

I'm the founder of an online company with a
humanistic, community-oriented vision, which
people experience right away when they come to
our site. They often write to me to express their
appreciation and I believe they are oblivious
to the fact that I am a Chinese-American female,
although there is a picture of me on the site.
Even if they consciously note that I'm a minority
woman, I believe that becomes inconsequential
since their first experience was their personal

interaction with the "essence" or personality of the site, and not with me.

My personal story is that the Internet has been a ticket to my professional freedom to pursue what I love to do in the way that I love to do it. It has enabled me to really reach out and touch our community throughout the world of middle-class "real people," even though I live in a very jaded high-tech environment. Also, because of the Net, I am able to work with a network of people throughout the country and there is tremendous flexibility in our creative and production process. For more details on this refer to: http://www.folksonline.com/folks/ts/story5/ story5.htm

I feel I am establishing relationships with people of all ages and walks of life whom I would rarely have the opportunity to interact with in my daily life in Silicon Valley. These are the folks of my roots: the middle class, middle America in which I grew up but left when I went off to college. I love to hear about their daily lives and their personal goals and dreams. It doesn't matter about the socioeconomic, educational, or cultural differences. That has been my experience on the Net and that's why I love it. I feel it's the medium that will bring about the experience of "oneness" for many of us, regardless of our race, gender, or other characteristics.

So instead of telling you about my unique experience as an Asian-American female online, I share with you my experience of relating with others on a human-being-to-human-being level. The Internet can be a tool to help women transcend the traditional barriers. I also would like to

encourage others who are "considered
disadvantaged" to take advantage of this
prejudice-free tool to go for what they want in
life. I am doing that, and so are thousands of
other women, minorities, handicapped, older folks,
and others. The Internet is the most powerful tool
available to anyone who can have access to the
Net, and one of my personal and professional goals
is to work on making it more accessible and
available to everyone.

Jan Zobel, a tax professional (enrolled agent) and author of *Minding Her Own Business: The Self-Employed Woman's Guide to Taxes and Recordkeeping*, uses the message board for the NAEA (National Association of Enrolled Agents). "Not only do we enrolled agents help each other with unusual tax problems and share 'weird stories,'" says Jan, "but there is a chat area where we discuss mundane things like the weather and what we're going to do after April 15. When we're working eighteen to twenty hours a day, having 'someone' who understands what our lives are like January to April is a real joy." Jan's book is also available online through online bookstores such as Amazon (http://www.amazon.com) and through the Small Business Adviser site (http://www.isquare.com).

As an entrepreneur, Leslie Birdsall gets advice for her own business and has extended her network of business advisers, supporters, and clients to whom she also gives business advice as a consultant to small businesses. "I have done work for women all over Canada and the United States, with paid clients as far away as Arizona to as close as my own backyard (Nova Scotia)," explains Leslie. "The opportunities to help and to make a difference to women who have or are hoping to have a business have provided me with personal and professional satisfaction and a sense of belonging that was not possible prior to this technology."

Karen Donahower is a hot-air balloon pilot and uses the Internet to pull up current weather and aviation-related data.

"Since I live in a very small town, when I fly locally it is very difficult to get accurate data from any location closer than fifty miles," says Karen. "Using the Weather Channel online [http://www.weather.com] and other aviation links, I can pull up instant radar summaries and pictures, I can get weather reports from towns as close as eight miles, and I can even access the FAA [http://www.faa.gov/] and the National Weather Service [http://www.nws.noaa.gov/] on the Web.

"Getting the most current information is critical. If not for Web access, some of the information I receive would be as much as eighteen hours old. In ballooning, where weather is everything, that is not good enough. I need to know what is happening at the moment, and what the forecast is for the day, so I can safely plan my flight and chart my flight path."

Says Marva Jackson, "The Internet has helped me to develop a home-based business enabling me to build a life for myself and my two-year-old daughter. I had been redefining my goals after having my baby and soon found that I was a single mom. The Internet has allowed me to develop a grassroots publicity service for independent Canadian artists, promoters, and nontraditional types of businesses, especially within the African Canadian communities." Marva learned all of her Internet skills by being online and sharing information with others online. She is one of the first black women in Canada to establish her own website (http://www.konekshuns.com/marvalous_konekshuns.html), and she had no technical expertise when she started.

April Barker, a fitness instructor, uses the Net to correspond with other fitness professionals around the world, to share ideas about motivation, choreography, sports nutrition, resources, and more. The Internet helps her stay current in the "ever-evolving world of fitness."

Elizabeth Kennedy graduated in May 1996, with minimal knowledge about computers. She moved to Seattle, got a job as a front-desk temp in a high-tech firm and, six months later, found herself editing the Industry Solutions sites at Microsoft. She's using the programming she has learned at work to create her own website and another site about ballroom dancing. Entirely self-taught, Elizabeth says the Internet "builds confidence, spurs creativity, and educates me."

With a degree in Russian and linguistics, Anne Baker (http://members.tripod.com/~Stasia/index.html) was planning on a career using Russian somehow, but she couldn't find a position after the breakup of the Soviet Union.

While working as a temporary secretary at a local college, she surfed the Net in her free time. She found some HTML tutorials on the Web, taught herself basic HTML, and found a place online where she could put up free Web pages. She then put up a site with her résumé and some of her husband's poetry. Later, she found some websites with job listings and sent out over a hundred résumés to tech companies in her area. She was hired the next week—without any formal training in computers or programming. "Everything I have learned about the Net, I have taught myself from the Net," says Anne.

As for using her Russian language skills, within the next five years she plans on starting her own consulting company in Russia. She wants to set up computer networking systems and teach people how to use computers and the Internet.

Chapter 18   Overcoming and Succeeding

Support in Tough Times

Women are using the Internet as a support network, a place where they can talk about their experiences, often anonymously, and get advice and encouragement from other people who have been through or are going through similar experiences. The Internet also connects women to a support system of friends and family during difficult times in their lives where they might have felt isolated.

Engeline Tan, a graphic designer, was recently separated from her husband, who had left her. "This resulted in my being very, very alone for a couple of months during which I surfed the Net a lot. It allowed me to stay alone and look more inside myself, yet meet new people, find old friends and teachers, and get back in touch with overseas family members in the Netherlands, Singapore, and Indonesia. I am now communicating with people I haven't seen since I was a child."

Beatrice Gilliam, a student studying art and anthropology with a special interest in Native Americans, is undergoing counseling with medication to treat manic depression. To her, the creative writing lists are especially important. She has found that the best way to deal with the changes in her life is to write about them and interact with writing groups online.

"Part of this process has involved telling stories about my childhood. This also prepares me for a book that I plan to write later in life. I want to write these things down before I lose the memories. Not only is this a great way to save my lore, but also I improve my writing skills!"

Beatrice also feels that the groups with whom she interacts on the Internet have helped her to improve her self-image and social skills. "Feedback is a source of power to me. In combination with the support from my husband and his family, the counseling, and the medication, the Internet has helped me resolve many issues," explains Beatrice. "I haven't started a business or run a support group through the wires, but I've managed to change my life for the better."

"The Net, I fully believe, saved my life," states Veronica Arnold (http://www.globalserve.net/~varnold). She had been extremely depressed and didn't know what was wrong. She was given a computer as a gift after asking for a new typewriter, and had spent the next year trying to learn how to use it.

Meanwhile, she became increasingly ill. She lost her balance, couldn't drive her car, her already bad hearing worsened, and her depression increased. She spent more time with the computer to keep from worrying about her condition and also because her mobility was becoming more and more restricted.

She discovered IRC (Internet relay chat) and made good friends online who helped her "just by being there. They did not know I was sick." Soon she was appointed as the "op" or "host" of the #help channel on IRC. She was able to help other people who were new to the Web—"newbies"—many of whom were scared and were looking for help online.

Then she had emergency brain surgery to remove a tumor. Her balance was restored, she was fitted with a hearing aid, and the quality of her life improved. She went on to build a website in partnership with someone she met online and is very comfortable with her computer now. She has added her watercolor gallery to her site and has sold three paintings off the site.

"I have gone from being a total recluse, and very ill, to enjoying people, and am now able to accept dinner speaking engagements about my art," Veronica explains, something that would have been "totally unthinkable" before. "I am proud of the progress I have made—from not knowing how to turn a computer on, to learning how to use it, learning HTML, and coping with my depression and illness—to the point of overcoming both, and now being fit, healthy, and happy."

Ellen Agger's mother was diagnosed with Alzheimer's disease in May 1996. Says Ellen: "After much searching for a support group in Toronto, I turned to the Internet." She searched for an online support group so she could use it whenever she wanted rather than having to wait for weekly meetings on the other side of town. She discovered a website called Caregiver Network (http://www.caregiver.on.ca).

There she found the support and information she needed and soon became a volunteer for the organization. She then learned to use PageMill (a software program for building websites) and later taught herself HTML. "I generally immersed myself in everything about Internet communication. I have since landed a part-time contract as Web coordinator for Alzheimer Canada, developing the content for their site [http://www.alzheimer.ca]."

The Internet helped Ellen find information quickly and research her mother's disease, even finding a site for an unusual type of Alzheimer's disease that her mother was being tested for. She found support for her "new, mind-blowing and life-changing role as a caregiver."

By the way, Ellen reports, "I only began becoming computer-literate two years ago. I was a health-care professional who had to have someone else open a file so I could type a report before all of this!"

Lisa Rodriguez was a single mother who was in an abusive relationship. She suffered from low self-esteem. Through her PC, she was able to reach out to others and, as she put it, "finally find the inner strength to get rid of the idiot I was with and find a better life for my son and me."

A year or so after being on America Online and meeting and talking to people, she received an Instant Message from a guy who thought they had a lot in common due to her online profile. At first she ignored him, but after several attempts, they finally had an online conversation that lasted close to two hours. After a month of daily emails and many online sessions, they decided to "talk live."

Their first phone conversation lasted three hours, and three weeks later, they had their first date. Over a year later, Lisa says, "He is absolutely wonderful and my self-esteem is at an all-time high. He is also great with my son, who hasn't had any contact with his biological father in about a year and a half. All in all it's a happy ending. I have a soul mate and my son has a positive male role model in his life. All due to America Online."

Taking Charge of Health

While some women find emotional support online to get them through difficult situations, other women find health information that helps them take charge of their lives. And women who are disabled in some way use the Internet as their connection to the world.

Jill Kennedy became familiar with the Internet and email through her consulting job. Then she bought a home computer and quickly began using the Internet to do research on her son's disease.

"My son, born April 13, 1993, has hypophosphatasia, which is a very rare genetic metabolic bone disease." Tells Jill: "There is only one doctor in the United States—at Shriner's Hospital Metabolic Research Unit in St. Louis—doing research on this disease, which affects about forty-five children in the United States. Shriner's policy does not allow the doctor to give out the names and addresses of other families affected with this disease; therefore, families must use other means to locate other families to share information and experiences."

Jill has used the Internet to locate several different support groups for families with children afflicted with rare or genetic diseases. Through the Internet, she has been referred to five families in the United States, England, and Bulgaria. She has also used the Net to check for any recently published articles on the disease. Through a posting on the Rare Genetic Diseases in Children Life-Link Topic Board, she has been contacted by seven families in the United States and Canada.

"In making contact with families, I have been able to match up a few families that have children with similar forms of the disease (two forms are fatal) so that they can provide each other with emotional support through very difficult times," Jill explains. "I have also been able to refer families to Shriner's Hospital for information or to participate in their ongoing research."

Newsgroups have had a big impact on Amy Cates's life. A project manager for an insurance company, Amy has suffered from an unknown disorder for seven years. Through newsgroups, she was able to find other people who had the same symptoms. Information she gathered online led her to return to her doctor to ask for a medication different from any she had previously tried. The request led her doctor to finding the perfect medication to treat her condition. "Now, after suffering seven years with little hope of relief, I am practically cured and able to live normally once again," says Amy. "This has and will continue to affect every area of my personal and professional life. It's like a miracle!"

Judi Lapsley-Miller, a Ph.D. candidate in psychophysics and psychology, also found information on the Internet that led to the diagnosis of a long-term illness.

"I had been unwell since a teenager, but the doctors had never sussed what was wrong," Judi explains. While reading the Usenet newsgroup sci.med, she read an article that described her symptoms. The description was about someone with fibromyalgia. She then did a search on the Web and found a large amount of information about this disease. According to Judi, many people suffer from fibromyalgia for years before they find out what is wrong.

"I had the diagnosis confirmed and have gotten the disease under control," says Judi. "I don't know anyone in my hometown who has this disease, but on Usenet, I have found hundreds. We all help each other to better understand the disease. Some of them have gone on to write books. There are also a number of doctors who visit alt.med.fibromyalgia and give sage advice. Given that I live in New Zealand, where we are often a bit behind on the latest treatments, I was able to make suggestions to my doctor about treatments. Nowadays I am coping well and have a far better quality of life."

"I have been into computers since I was fourteen," says Heather Wheless. "I loved trying to one-up my friends and write cool programs; however, I had never thought of turning to the Internet to answer some serious questions until after being online for several years."

Heather has had rheumatoid arthritis since she was eighteen months old. Although she hadn't suffered much in grade school, when she got to college, it got worse. She didn't really know how to deal with the changes in her body, how to get to class when she couldn't walk, how to get up and down the stairs to her dorm room, how to walk down the hall to the showers when she had severe morning stiffness.

"I finally wised up and got on alt.support.arthritis [a Usenet newsgroup]." Heather actually had to put in a petition to her school to get access to all the support "alt" Usenet newsgroups, which the school had blocked, just to access important medical information.

"Online, I learned to use crutches when my ankles weren't ready to go, but I needed to go. I got a lot of support and caring and understanding through that newsgroup. I could talk with other women with arthritis about what shoes I should wear to go on an interview. Sounds dumb, but it is an issue when you need high-tops for ankle support, but, of course, that would never do with a serious interview dress. I learned lots of things from the group and couldn't have made it this far without them."

Donna Manvich, a copyright researcher and permissions acquisitions specialist, was able to start her own home-based business through the New York State Department of Education, VESID (Vocational and Educational Services for Individuals with Disabilities). She started SourceLink, Inc., and won the Multiple Sclerosis Achievement Award in 1996. To exchange ideas and stories, she visits various websites to meet other people with disabilities, including the chatrooms at the site for Massachusetts General Hospital and Harvard University Medical School Department of Neurology.

Says Donna: "I have found it best to converse with individuals who have the same disability [as I]. The reason for this is camaraderie, lack of having to explain the disease, etc., and most important, real honest to goodness help!!" Other sites Donna has found helpful include the National MS Society (http://www.nmss.org/), National MS Society in New York (http://www.msnyc.org/) and Colorado, Albert Einstein College of Medicine (http://www.aecom.yu.edu/), Columbia Presbyterian in New York (http://cpmcnet.columbia.edu/), and the

Mayo Clinic (http://www.mayo.edu). "The Web has not only brought me into contact with many people suffering with MS whom I feel comfortable with, it has allowed me to stay on the cutting edge of research results and world studies going on regarding this disease."

For Brandi Jasmine, a freelance writer, illustrator, and astrologer, the Net is sometimes the only way she can have contact with others. "I have physical limitations and allergies to smoke and alcohol, as well as other environmental sensitivities, so the Internet helps me make connections, stay in touch, and meet people I might never have met otherwise." The Net has also helped her career. "Virtually all my contacts, suppliers, and markets have come to me online. I have met business associates and made contacts in my field that I would not have had access to in the offline community."

Chapter 19 Educators and Activists

Rachelle Wolosoff, an elementary school teacher currently doing graduate work, is in email contact with another teaching student in another state, and they discuss teaching methods and issues in their respective parts of the country.

Jane Jordan, also a teacher, says that "the Internet has given me an opportunity to learn from teachers all over the world. It gives unlimited sources for my students, and has allowed me to set up pen pals for my students."

May Leong, an instructor at a graduate university in Japan and a self-proclaimed "computer/Net newbie," describes her current situation. "Being located three hours north of Tokyo, I'm surrounded by rice fields, mountains, a small university—population 200+ students and 100 faculty/staff. I'm isolated from the English language and the world at large." The Net allows May to find out about and keep up with the news on a daily basis and to gather articles and lists of sites for her students.

Laura Bashlor, a fifty-eight-year-old middle-school teacher in the Midwest, feels that computers and the Internet have changed her life, making her more excited about teaching every day. While her contemporaries are retiring, she says she feels that she's in the prime of life.

Laura remembers back to twelve years ago, when the parents' club bought the first computers for the elementary school where she was teaching. "Almost all of the teachers stayed far away from these machines and continued to teach as before," she recalls. "Their attitude appalled me, and I did the opposite, taking a computer home each weekend until I could afford one for myself."

Her attitude toward the computers forged a unique place for her in the school district. She added simple programming in LOGO to her second-grade curriculum. Three years ago, she accepted the challenge of middle school. Soon after, there was a phone line in her classroom for her modem. "We had and still have the only Internet connection in the district," says Laura. "Soon, however, our school network will be online and my position will be even more valuable. Without computers and the Internet I would be just another burned-out teacher counting the days until retirement."

From: Susan Geller Ettenheim, cybrarian
http://www.femina.com/

The Net has empowered my life in an amazing way. Just a year ago, I was in a traditional part-time library position, struggling to balance my life as a visual artist, my family, and a paying job, while taking computer classes at night. I was searching to develop a new skill that would allow me freedom to work from different locations and flexibility of hours. I was hoping to combine experience in the fine arts, teaching/research experience, some freelance writing experience, and my knowledge of books.

On the Internet, I am now developing a base of work that has much of the flexibility I wanted, great challenges in being on the cutting edge of new Internet research possibilities and teaching opportunities, and the opening of a whole new world of visual/art opportunities. In addition, I am also now empowered by the discovery that not only can I use the Internet, but I am capable of and even enjoy fixing technical problems that arise with the software and hardware!

Kathy Watkins, creator of the Activist's Oasis website (http://www.matisse.net/~kathy/activist/activist.html), made her first website in the summer of 1994. She was working as administrative director at CARAL (http://www.caral.org), a pro-choice nonprofit organization, and the first thing she put on the Web was a 1994 voter guide so people would know which candidates were pro- or anti-choice.

She had had an email account since 1988, so she had been

following the development of the Internet and the World Wide Web with an eye toward how these technologies could be used to help struggling nonprofits multiply their efforts. Her roommate taught her the basics of HTML, and together they held seminars to help activists get online and benefit from the Internet.

In 1995, she quit her job and started working as a freelance Web consultant, creating sites for both for-profit and not-for-profit groups. She also teaches other nonprofits how to create their own websites through classes at the Support Center for Nonprofit Management in San Francisco.

Ann Fonfa is a volunteer at SHARE. She calls herself a (breast) cancer survivor/activist and signs all of her email "Ann Fonfa, not a born cynic." She graduated from Pace University at the age of thirty, with a B.A. in professional studies, a life-learning degree, with a major in sales and marketing. "I loved being in school at that age, having dropped out of three other colleges in the sixties," says Ann. "I was deeply involved with the antiwar movement, civil rights, and then women's rights."

In 1992, she worked as a salesperson for a computer graphics firm and they gave her her first computer. She joined Women's Wire (a now-defunct national online service for women) from an advertisement in a women's newspaper.

She discovered live chat, and her first month online cost $149 (in the days before flat rates online). "I used the Internet extensively to research health issues. I joined various talk groups and had tons of email. I was busy all the time on the computer and welcomed those evenings when I couldn't sleep since I could use the computer time."

In April 1995, she worked on putting together information about breast cancer on the national BBS Women's Wire. She also was a guest on a chat on America Online about alternative breast cancer treatments. She has put an announcement online about a treatment she had been using for her breast cancer, and several people responded with requests for more information. "It was exciting to exchange news of my success with them," says Ann.

Chapter 20 Women Doing Research

Judy Hinkes Zeddies, a former desktop publisher, made a sudden career change. She went back to school to become a pastry chef. She bought a home computer to do her homework and was introduced to the Web.

"I use the Web to research recipes and food history and have met other 'foodies' through forums and lists. The Net has allowed me to do my research with much wider sources of info than my local [Chicago public] library has. Also, the speed of return is incredible, allowing me to continue working because I can do research into the wee hours if necessary. I have also used the Net to research product pricing for my restaurant management coursework to figure food-cost percentages. There are also terrific nutrition sites, including the American Dietetic Association [http://www.eatright.org/]."

Melle Baker, a twenty-one-year-old theater studies major, has researched "everything from sexual harassment to still-life art to natural science, psychology, and theater history" online, and she loves "the ease and variety of the Internet." Recently, she did research for several term papers, including one about the Clarence Thomas confirmation hearings and Anita Hill's testimony and another about the links between sexual stereotypes and witchcraft as seen in Anne Rice's characters. She looks up authors she likes and has even found books online that she had trouble finding in the real world. She also researches information for her parents, especially for their vacations.

As a fiction writer and marketing and PR consultant, Jeannie Dodson-Edgars uses the Internet for everything from tracking and accessing mutual fund data to subscribing to newspapers and news services as well as sending letters to the editors at newspapers.

Her use of the Net for research has covered topics ranging from ancient mythology (8500–3500 B.C.E.) to public funding of the arts. "The Net is a worldwide library. I can find something on any topic I am interested in from energy efficiencies, irrigation equipment, to Great Goddess mythology, and gain access to university libraries," says Jeannie.

Rachel Wade, a college sophomore, has done Web research on numerous subjects including Latin American politics for a model United Nations, the status of women in Algeria for French class, women in politics for math class (oddly enough), and the Cinderella story and women in fairy tales for a novel she is writing. She has also researched body piercing at the rec.arts.bodyart Usenet newsgroup, something she is considering but wanted information about it first.

Rachel subscribes to several Internet mailing discussion lists, one about the singer Ani DiFranco, which usually gives her access to information on the artist before the general public gets it, and on another list for folk deejays, which, Rachel explains, "has enabled me to learn how other deejays structure their shows, and also to hear about and get CDs of new and often unadvertised music which our tiny and cash-strapped radio station desperately needs."

Kristi Kattapong describes herself as a perpetual student, currently a doctoral candidate in applied social psychology, but "trying to ease myself into the workforce." She uses the Internet to get travel information, to research academic papers, to research video documentary projects, and to get networking information.

Chapter 21   Hobbyists and Travelers

From: Wendy Bumgardner, walker

My hobby is walking. I participate in volksmarches—10-kilometer noncompetitive walking events. These walks are held to promote healthy activity. For the past 12 years I have been walking, joined a club, and rose through the ranks to national VP of the American Volkssport Association. I played on the online services—Prodigy, GEnie, America Online—and enjoyed chatting about walking (as well as frequenting the Star Trek forums). When the Web first became available 2 years ago, I decided that the AVA needed a website to publicize our clubs and events. I got a personal account and learned website creation from scratch. In the last few months more of our 500 clubs are deciding to join in with their own websites or add their information to our site at http://www.teleport.com/~walking/.

Melissa Bell taught herself HTML and designed her own website, which she called The Celestial Circle (http://www.geocities.com/Athens/5224). "I'm very interested in New Age philosophies and wanted to meet people with similar ideas, so I started my own online club as well as a club in my city. I'm also an English major and use my website to showcase my poetry. The Internet provides a spiritual outlet for me that my hometown could not," she explains.

Gail Hughes's favorite pastime is gardening. She discovered a website for swapping seed. "Through seed exchanges, I have developed some great friendships with people in several countries and have added new and interesting plants to my collection, while learning about other cultures and people," says Gail.

She also participates in gardening chats on specific gardening sites such as the Garden Escape Chat Room (http://www.garden.com) and sends flowers to people by way of the Virtual Florist (http://www.virtualflorist.com).

Roberta Gross is sixty years old, and although her husband and children spend hours in front of their computer, checking their email and their stock portfolios, initially she couldn't find a use for the computer or the Internet. The only time she had shown any interest was when she was searching for a recipe for shepherd's pie for her youngest son, as it was his favorite dish and she wanted to make it for him. She asked a friend to search for her, and together they found all kinds of recipes for shepherd's pie: vegetarian, Irish, Indian, and, of course, the one she was looking for: English. The next weekend, her son Eric had shepherd's pie for dinner.

But recipes weren't really enough to keep her interested in the Internet, and she didn't go back to the computer again for a long while—until she started playing bridge. Roberta discovered that there was a way to play bridge on the Internet. "You mean there are other people out there playing actual bridge together over the computer?" she asked her son and daughter-in-law. "How does that work? Show me." Today, Roberta has finally mastered the art of double-clicking, has made friends in Norway through her bridge playing, and is now shopping the computer stores for a laptop of her very own.

Elana Lindquist, a nontechnical person and teacher, was so excited about the Web that she wrote a series of articles for a newspaper called "My Adventures on the Web" (http://www.execpc.com/~elanal/My_Adventures.html), sharing how she used the Web for house hunting, moving across the country two times, and making friends.

When Elana was relocating to Franklin, Wisconsin, from Spokane, Washington, she went to the University of Milwaukee's website, where she made two pen pals who helped her make the transition. She also looked up Wisconsin real estate sites and found a real estate agent who worked with her and her

husband to find their dream house. She was able to look at listings of homes online. When they were about to purchase their
house, Elana was able to find the latest information about mort-
gage rates on the Internet.

From: Elana

I have two school-age children. This past week my
daughter Nicole, age 13, had homework on outer
space. We were able to go directly to NASA and the
United Nations for help. When I had difficulty
finding information about it I quickly emailed help
at NASA and got an answer back the next day from a
very gracious person. Another time this year she
needed up-to-date information about the environment
in India. We were able to go to a library in India
to find what we needed. No library in this
community could have provided us with the quality
of information we were able to get in our own home
in a short time using the Internet.

In short, I find the Internet to be an exciting
tool to use to enrich and broaden lives. No longer
are we limited by the resources of our community.
No longer are we controlled by the information
we can read in our local papers or libraries
or bookstores, or learn from our teachers and
friends. We are crossing a new frontier where
borders don't exist and where everyone can
participate.

Zibby Wilder claims the Net made her dream vacation to
Ecuador and the Galápagos Islands come true. "I bought discounted plane tickets online, located hostels, found information
on culture and customs, and learned what towns to visit and how
to get there," tells Zibby. "I spent the entire month of Decem-
ber discovering a place I knew nothing about, armed with only a

guidebook and the amazing amount of information I uncovered or was provided with through the Web. What an amazing time-saving, people-friendly resource!"

Five months before her trip, she went to the search engines and found the following useful sites:

South American Explorers Club
http://www.samexplo.org/
For travelers to Ecuador, Peru, and surrounding countries, visiting this website and becoming a member of the club is a must! "Our trip would have been a disaster without this resource."

The Internet Guide to Hostelling
http://www.hostels.com/
Good, recent info on this bulletin board on good places to eat and stay—cheap.

The Lonely Planet Online
http://www.lonelyplanet.com/
The online version of the worldwide guide books. Gives good overviews on destinations.

Latin World
http://www.latinworld.com
Good, general info on destinations and travel in Latin America.

The Simple Traveler
http://www.simpletraveler.com/
Some fun views on travel and documenting trips.

Internet Travel Network
http://www.itn.net/
"I booked cheap flights through a travel consolidator I found here. They also gave me really good advice on the benefits of booking flights (to Galápagos, etc.) from within Ecuador rather than from the United States.

"And of course, I got some great info and answers to difficult questions from other travelers and even local residents on rec.travel.latin-america and soc.culture.latin-america."

For Molly Koranda, a very useful application online was the Amtrak bulletin board on Prodigy. "My family was taking a cross-country trip on Amtrak and there must be some third-shift employees with time on their hands because I always had the latest, most accurate information regarding Amtrak schedules."

Chapter 22   Girls on the Web

I always stress the importance of making sure that girls do not get left behind when it comes to math, science, and technology. Girls need fun and interesting places to go online so they are entertained, educated, and inspired. There are many personal websites created by girls where their personality comes across and they get the chance to express themselves.

One of the ways girls have been included in technology and business is through Take Our Daughters to Work Days, which are held once a year around the country. You can find out more about the project at http://www.ms.foundation.org/todindex.html and see photographs from recent events at http://www.dcweb grrls.org/daughters and http://inbox.timeinc.com/daughter.

From: Heather MacEachern, student

I am 17 years old, and a student. I taught myself html when I was 15 and have been online for about 2 years now. I started a small website for my favorite band, Sloane (http://www.webgate.net/~ maenon/sloan), with a friend of mine. It has now gone on to be their official website and we get over 60 visitors a day, although I still do this for free. Also, I am an amateur photographer and photographed many bands. On my personal website I have a list of all the bands I have photos of and links to their sites, and scans of my photos.

Jennifer, eleven
http://www.enter.net/~blair/jenypage/jenypage.html
She has a hermit crab named Browning and loves gymnastics, playing the piano, listening to music, and her computer.

Carol, thirteen
http://carol.tierranet.com/
She loves Winnie the Pooh—her favorite animal is Piglet. Her favorite show on TV is *Sabrina the Teenage Witch*. She

also likes to hang out with her friends, shop, sew, watch TV, and swim.

Amanda, eleven
http://www.geocities.com/SoHo/Gallery/5446/

Amanda's site has artwork that she has created on the computer. She says she likes fairies, flowers, teddy bears, tea, Christmas, animals, roses, peaches, peach-flavored candy, vanilla ice cream, moons and stars, lip gloss, snowflakes, the color blue, rain, winter, and summer.

Jeni, sixteen
http://macatawa.org/~jeni/

With great art that she creates herself, Jeni says she likes working on her Web page, exploring the Internet, hanging out with her friends and family, learning new things (scuba diving and playing the guitar), peanut M&M's, summer, reading, eating, sleeping, and thinking.

Mary, thirteen
http://members.aol.com/Hov/index4.html

Mary loves music and movies, and her favorite TV shows include *The Brady Bunch*, *I Love Lucy*, *Sabrina the Teenage Witch*, and *Friends*. She hates tornadoes, algebra, seafood, and snobs.

Katherine Torski, twelve (and her dad)
http://www.eci.com/torski/

Katherine loves horses, cooking, learning to play piano and violin, and Beanie Babies, especially Waddle. She plays soccer, reads, and skates.

Quick List of Girl-Friendly Sites

American Girl
http://www.americangirl.com

Sharing the experience of what it's like to grow up as a girl in America with an exclusive American girls club, and a magazine just for girls, as well as an events calendar and a catalog of ways to show off your pride of being an American girl.

Girls Incorporated
http://www.girlsinc.org/
Girls Incorporated is a national youth organization dedicated to helping every girl become strong, smart, and bold. Includes a campaign for girls to Stamp Out Smoking.

Girl Power
http://www.girlpower.com/
A site to encourage and motivate young women toward creative self-expression, specifically through writing.

Girlspace
http://www.girlspace.com
The truth about puberty and periods—brought to you by Kotex.

Kristi Yamaguchi
http://www.kristi.org
Has an in-line skating fundraiser to raise money for the Always Dream Foundation to help young children.

New Moon
http://www.newmoon.org/
An online and print magazine for girls and their dreams, written by girls.

Planet Girl
http://www.planetgirl.com
Here you can chat, read their newsletter, play games, follow an online comic strip, or buy things at their store.

Purple Moon
http://www.purple-moon.com
From the makers of CD Roms for girls, a place where you can meet other girls.

TeenSpeak
http://www.teenspeak.com/
Created by teen Leslie Ann Jones for teens to speak their mind on topics from fashion, music, literature, and relationships to movies, pets, sports, religion, and poetry.

Chapter 23   The Future

What does the future hold for women online? With technology changing so rapidly, it's hard to predict what tomorrow's Internet will be like or if we'll have Interactive TV. I think it's safe to say that, knowing how quickly the Internet has grown and how the number of women online has increased, the Internet will be an integral communications tool in all of our lives, and that women will have a strong presence online.

When trying to imagine the type of technology tools we'll use in the future, I've always envisioned some kind of big screen on the wall of every home that taps into television, where you can select what shows you want to watch and when, where you can order your groceries to be delivered to your door, where you can do research, talk to friends and family, and view videos of your vacation destination before booking your flight. Sort of a one-stop shopping for all that women do in their everyday lives.

In order for women to gain and maintain a strong position in the technology and new media industries and to be the creators of the technologies, girls have to be encouraged early to get involved in math, science, and computers. We each have to act as role models for all girls as well as for other women, showing them that technology isn't something to fear but something to control and utilize for their benefit.

Take the time to learn something new about computers or the Internet. Then take the time to teach another woman or girl what you have learned. If we each help one other woman get online, we'll build a legacy of technical savvy and connectedness to the world for our daughters and granddaughters.

APPENDIXES

Cybergrrl Resources on the Web

Cybergrrl Satellite Sites

Cybergrrl Webstation
http://www.cybergrrl.com/
The main entrance to all the sites in the Cybergrrl Webstation.

The Adventures of Cybergrrl
http:/www.cybergrrl.com/planet/comic/
An online comic strip with five female superheroes.

Cybergrrl Village
http://village.cybergrrl.com
The first Web-based online service with chat, posting boards, quick messaging, a Who's Here button to see who is on the site with you, personal profiles, and free home pages.

Planet Cybergrrl
http://www.cybergrrl.com/planet/
Cybergrrl is "Your guide to going online" and this site reviews cool sites, has a regular Cybergrrl column, and the "Adventures of Cybergrrl" comic strip as well as links to a book site, travel site, and more!

Webgrrls
http://www.webgrrls.com/
Online and offline networking for women who are interested in the Internet or learning about computers and technology.

Femina
http://www.femina.com/
The first searchable directory of female-friendly websites.

MondoGirl
http://www.mondogirl.com/
The hub for girls' information, community, and fun online.

Bookgrrl
http://.www.bookgrrl.com/
Books for, by, and about women.

Travelgrrl
http://www.travelgrrl.com/
The perfect travel companion for the woman traveler.

WomenZone
http://www.womenzone.com/
Like a magazine online for women, only you can "talk back" and express your own ideas and opinions about the issues.

The Amazing Webgrrls

The Webgrrls Mission: Webgrrls is an international networking group that helps women succeed in an increasingly technical workplace and world by providing a forum for women who are interested in the Internet to exchange job and business leads, mentor and teach, intern and learn.

There are Webgrrls chapters around the world. To find the most up-to-date listing of Webgrrls chapters, go to http://www. webgrrls.com/howgrrl.html. To start a chapter, send email to @cgim.com for more information.

Northeast, USA
Five Colleges (Amherst, Hampshire, Mount Holyoke, Smith and UMass-Amherst)
website: http://hamp.hampshire.edu/~5grrl
email: 5 colleges@webgrrls.com

Boston, Massachusetts
website: http://www.gen.com/bos-webgrrls
email: boston@webgrrls.com

Capital District (Albany, New York)
website: http://webgrrls.com/capital/
email: albany@webgrrls.com

Connecticut
website: http://webgrrls.c.maagnum.com/
email: danbury@webgrrls.com
newhaven@webgrrls.com
stamford@webgrrls.com

Cyburbia, New Jersey
website: http://www.webgrrls.com/cyburbia/
email: cyburbianj@webgrrls.com.

Ithaca, New York
website: http://www.webgrrls.com/ithaca/
email: ithaca@webgrrls.com

Jersey City, New Jersey
website: pending
email: jerseycity@webgrrls.com

Long Island, New York
website: http://www.bworks.com/wgli
email: li@webgrrls.com

New York City
website: http://www.webgrrls.com/ny/index.html
email: nyc@webgrrls.com
If you are in NYC, call 212-642-8012 and leave your name and
phone number.

Philadelphia, Pennsylvania
website: pending
email: philly@webgrrls.com

Pittsburgh, Pennsylvania
website: pending
email: pittsburgh@webgrrls.com

Staten Island, New York
website: pending
email: si@webgrrls.com

Mid-Atlantic
Washington, D.C.
website: http://www.dcwebgrrls.org
email: dc@webgrrls.com

The Southeast
Atlanta, Georgia
website: http://www.webgrrls.com/atlanta/
email: atlanta@webgrrls.com

Chattanooga, Tennessee
website: pending
email: chattanooga@webgrrls.com

Columbia, South Carolina
website: pending
email: columbiasc@webgrrls.com

Ft. Lauderdale, Florida
website: http://www.webgrrls.com/ftlauderdale
email: ftlaud@webgrrls.com

Jacksonville, Florida
website: http://www.jaxflorida.com/webgrrls/
email: jaxfla@webgrrls.com

Raleigh/Durham/Chapel Hill, North Carolina (Triangle)
website: http://www.trianglewebgrrls.com/
email: triangle@webgrrls.com

Space Coast, Florida (East Coast)
website: http://www.webgrrls.com/spacecoast/
email: spacecoast@webgrrls.com

Tampa, Florida (Sun Coast)
website: http://www.cyberelf.com/webgrrls
email: tampa@webgrrls.com

Virginia Beach/Hampton Roads, Virginia
website: pending
email: vabeach@webgrrls.com

Midwest

Akron, Ohio
website: http://www.2theweb.com/webgrrls
email: akron@webgrrls.com

Billings, Montana
website: pending
email: billings@webgrrls.com

Chicago, Illinois
website: http://www.xsite.net/~webgrrls
email: chicago@webgrrls.com

Cincinnati, Ohio
website: http://webgrrls-cincinnati.com/
email: cincy@webgrrls.com

Columbia, Missouri (mid-Missouri)
website: pending
email: columbiamo@webgrrls.com

Columbus, Ohio
website: http://www.webgrrls.com/columbus/
email: columbusoh@webgrrls.com

Denver, Colorado
website: http://members.aol.com/riznsun/grrls
email: denver@webgrrls.com

Detroit, Michigan
website: http://www.webgrrls.com/motorcity/
email: motorcity@webgrrls.com

Flint, Michigan
website: pending
email: flint@webgrrls.com

Iowa (Council Bluffs, Iowa, and Eastern Nebraska)
website: pending
email: iowa@webgrrls.com

Minneapolis/St. Paul, Minnesota (Twin Cities)
website: http://www.webgrrls.com/tc/
email: twincities@webgrrls.com

Oklahoma City, Oklahoma
website: http://www.webgrrls.com/okcity/
email: okcity@webgrrls.com

Southeastern Wisconsin
website: http://www.execpc.com/~arana/grrls.html
email: sewisconsin@webgrrls.com

Tulsa, Oklahoma
website: pending
email: tulsa@webgrrls.com

Northwest
Ketchikan, Alaska
website: http://puffin.ptialaska.net/~jgoforth/wgindex.html
email: ketchikan@webgrrls.com

Boise, Idaho
website: http://www.webgrrls.com/boise/
email: boise@webgrrls.com

Seattle, Washington
website: http://www.ixa.net/~grrl/
email: seattle@webgrrls.com

Southwest
Albuquerque, New Mexico
website: http://www.webgrrls.com/albuquerque/
email: albuquerque@webgrrls.com

Austin, Texas
website: http://www.amy.com/webgrrls/
email: austin@webgrrls.com

Dallas, Texas
website: http://www.bbgun.com/webgrrls/
email: dallas@webgrrls.com

Ft. Worth, Texas
website: http://members.aol.com/FTWwebgrrl/home.html
email: ftworth@webgrrls.com

Houston, Texas
website: http://www.freshpages.com/webgrrls
email: houston@webgrrls.com

Phoenix, Arizona
website: http://www.webgrrls.com/phoenix/
email: phoenix@webgrrls.com

Tucson, Arizona
website: pending
email: tucson@webgrrls.com

Salt Lake City, Utah
website: pending
email: slc@webgrrls.com

West Coast and Hawaii
Central Coast, California (Monterey, Santa Cruz)
website: http://www.webgrrls.com/cc/
email: cc@webgrrls.com

Los Angeles, California
website: http://www.webgrrls.com/la/
email: la@webgrrls.com

Sacramento, California
website: http://www.webgrrls.com/sacramento/
email: sacramento@webgrrls.com

San Diego, California
website: http://www.webgrrls.com/sandiego/
email: sandiego@webgrrls.com

San Francisco, California
website: http://www.webgrrls.com/sf/
email: sanfran@webgrrls.com

Silicon Valley, California
website: http://www.webgrrls.com/sv/
email: sv@webgrrls.com

Honolulu, Hawaii
website: http://www.webgrrls.com/hawaii/
email: honolulu@webgrrls.com

Maui, Hawaii
website: http://www.webgrrls.com/hawaii/
email: maui@webgrrls.com

Canada

Kelowna, British Columbia
website: pending
email: kelownabc@webgrrls.com

London, Ontario (Forest City)
website: http://www.info.london.on.ca/webgrrls/
email: londonont@webgrrls.com

Mississauga, Ontario
website: http://www.webgrrls.com/mssauga/
email: mssauga@webgrrls.com

Montreal, Quebec
website: http://www.webgrrls.com/montreal
email: montreal@webgrrls.com

Niagara Region, Ontario
website: http://www.webgrrls.niagara.com
email: niagaraont@webgrrls.com

North Halton/North Peel, Ontario
website: pending
email: tanya@stn.net

Ottawa, Ontario
website: http://www.webgrrls.com/ottawa/
email: ottawa@webgrrls.com

Toronto, Ontario
website: http://www.webgrrls.com/toronto/
email: toronto@webgrrls.com

United Kingdom
London, England
website: pending
email: londonuk@webgrrls.com

Dublin, Ireland
website: pending
email: dublin@webgrrls.com

Europe
Belgium
website: http://www.dma.be/p/webgrrls/index.htm
email: benelux@webgrrls.com

Denmark (Aathus)
website: pending
email: aathus@webgrrls.com

Denmark (Copenhagen)
website: http://www.webgrrls.dk/
email: copenhagen@webgrrls.com

Germany
website: http://www.webgrrls.de/
email: germany@webgrrls.com

Greece (Athens)
website: pending
email: athens@webgrrls.com

Italy (Milan)
website: http://www.italynet.com/webgrrls
email: italy@webgrrls.com

Netherlands
website: http://www.mediaport.org/~webgrrls/
email: netherlands@webgrrls.com

Sweden
website: pending
email: sweden@webgrrls.com

Down Under and Beyond

Barbados, West Indies
website: pending
email: barbados@webgrrls.com

Brisbane, Australia
website: http://www.powerup.com.au/~qldq/webgrrls.html
email: brisbane@webgrrls.com

Canberra, Australia
website: pending
email: canberra@webgrrls.com

Christchurch, New Zealand
website: http://www.ch.planet.gen.nz/~women/webgrrls/
email: christchurch@webgrrls.com

Melbourne, Australia
website: http://www.home.aone.net.au/webgrrls/
email: melbourne@webgrrls.com

Puerto Rico
website: pending
email: pr@webgrrls.com

Capetown, South Africa
website: http://www.webgrrlssa.co.za
email: capetown@webgrrls.com

Sydney, Australia
website: http://www.webgrrls.com/sydney/
email: sydney@webgrrls.com

Wellington, Aotearoa, New Zealand
website: http://www.webgrrls.org.nz
email: wellington@webgrrls.com

Western Australia
website: pending
email: westaustralia@webgrrls.com

Asia
Manila, Philippines
website: pending
email: manila@webgrrls.com

Hong Kong, China
website: http://www.webgrrls.com/hk/
email: hongkong@webgrrls.com

Tokyo, Japan
website: http://www.iuj.ac.jp/webgrrls
email: tokyo@webgrrls.com

If You Are in Another City
You can start your own Webgrrls℠ group. Just email start@cgim.com or call 212-642-8012 for permission, guidelines, and other details and specify where you are located in the "Subject" of your email. We will send you information via email only.

If You Are in College, Join Webgrrls on Campus
http://www.webgrrls.com/campus/

Glossary

agents Also called intelligent agents or bots, special software that performs an "intelligent" function such as going out onto the World Wide Web and indexing all the new sites for a search engine or remembering what your favorite music is and then "making" recommendations to you based on your previous choices.

archie Internet software tool that searches FTP databases for big files such as games, software upgrades, and fonts.

ascii (pronounced: 'as-key) American Standard Code for Information Interchange. A standard for upper- and lowercase letters, numbers, and symbols on computers.

bandwidth The size of the "pipe" or how much room the electric wires have on which to transmit data. Big graphics take up a lot of bandwidth, which is why websites with big graphics take longer to load than text, which takes up very little bandwidth. If you talk too much online or talk about off-topic things on a list, you might be told by someone to "stop wasting bandwidth."

BBS Bulletin Board System. A computer that is set up with several modems to allow other computers to log into it. BBSs can be for games, research, or communication on topics ranging from health to science to cooking.

bit Binary digit, a one or a zero. The smallest unit that makes up computerized data.

bookmark On your Web browser, you can save a place in the browser to a site you've visited that you want to return to so you don't have to write down the address. The browser remembers.

bot Also known as an "agent" or "intelligent agent." See *agents*.

bozo filter The term for special software or a special command you can use to block inappropriate conversations online from troublemakers.

browser   Or Web browser. Your "window to the Web"— the piece of software on your computer that helps you see the different pieces of a website, combining graphics, text, and other files.

bps   Bits per second. How fast data are transferred electronically. A 14.4 modem sends and receives data traveling at 14,400 bits per second; 28.8 modems move data at the speed of 28,800 bps.

byte   Binary term. A set of bits that make up a single character in computer processing: 8 bits = 1 byte; 1000 bits = 1 kilobyte; 1 million bits = 1 megabyte. On your modem, 14.4 or 28.8 Kbps is how speed is measured—how fast the modem transfers data.

comm port   The communications port or the outlet on the side or back of your computer where you plug in an external modem.

COS   Commercial online service. A company that offers online access through their own computer network. Examples of the biggest are America Online (AOL), CompuServe, Prodigy, and the Microsoft Network (MSN).

cpu   The central processing unit of your computer— usually the big box that also contains the hard drive. The speed that your computer processes information is measured in megahertz.

cursor   The spot where your mouse can point or you can enter data into a word-processing program. When you are using a Web browser, your cursor is actually an arrow, but in a word processing program, your cursor is a vertical line that blinks.

cyberspace   The term for the nebulous "space" created by loosely networked computers. First used by William Gibson in his book *Neuromancer*.

database   A searchable collection of data or information and the way information is organized on the Internet— in databases such as FTP, Gopher, and the World Wide Web.

dial-up access   When you access the Internet or an online service by dialing up through your modem, it's dial-up access. When you are at work and can access the

Internet without having to dial a number, you have a different kind of access, usually a faster access through a T–1 connection.

domain name The name of a server or computer on the Internet that replaces the IP address, which is more like a computer's zip code. Cybergrrl.com is the domain name, while 19.306.38.07 is an example of an IP address.

download To retrieve information from another computer and save it onto your own computer. Opposite is to upload.

email Electronic mail. Digital letters that you can send over the phone lines through the Internet.

emoticons Little symbols you use in email and electronic postings to express emotions such as :-), which is a smile and :-(, which is a frown.

Ethernet A way of networking computers within an office. With an Ethernet connection, you can often get onto the Internet without having to dial up an access provider like you do with a dial–up account.

FAQ Frequently asked questions. Usually a file or document on a website or in a forum that answers some of the most often asked questions about the forum or topic.

filters In your email software program, filters can help you sort through your email, filtering them into separate email boxes for organization's sake.

finger Internet software tool that finds people and their online profiles. Often includes a log of when they've been online. Usually a compilation of information given by you to your *ISP*, so make sure you know how to access this and edit it in case you want to change the information the public sees.

flame An angry email or post in response to something you or someone else has said or done. When you do not behave appropriately online, you are bound to be flamed (see *netiquette*).

forum A forum can simply be a posting board, messaging board, or bulletin board where people leave messages and have conversations. Or a forum can refer to a collection of resources on a single topic such as a travel forum, which might have a posting board, a chatroom, and several articles to read.

Freenet   Another way to get online—a company or group who has created an online network that offers free access to members of the community. Sometimes state-funded.

FTP   File transfer protocol. The act of transferring files via the Internet using FTP software and going into FTP databases or sites.

gateway   The opening onto the Internet. For example, America Online is essentially a closed network system open only to members, but it does have a gateway out to the Internet so members can access the Web. Corporate networks sometimes have a gateway to the Internet for email use or Web access, but not always.

GIF   Graphics interchange format. A type of graphics file that is most commonly used on the World Wide Web.

gopher   The act of searching files via the Internet using Gopher software and going into Gopher databases, which consist of text-only files.

GUI   Graphical user interface. The graphics, buttons, pictures, and other visual cues that give a site its "look and feel" and help you navigate through it more easily. Not text-only.

hacker   A person who likes to break into computer systems or "hack" them to get to private information.

hard drive   The storage room of your computer. It holds the data or information even when the computer is off.

hardware   The hard, tangible "stuff" of computers—the monitor, the CPU, and the cables and cords. Like your house, the walls of your house, and the electrical wiring.

home page   The first page of a website, the opening page someone arrives at upon first entering a site.

host   Usually, host refers to the server or computer that "hosts" an online service or a website.

HTML	Hypertext markup language—the "language of websites." Easy programming that creates links on the page and embeds graphics, sound, and other files into the text.
http	Hypertext transfer protocol—the "language of the World Wide Web." This precedes every Web address and means that the information in the site conforms to Web protocol.
hypertext	The term used to describe the linking of text from one document to another, either within the same site or database or to a site somewhere in the world.
Internet	"Internetworked" computers around the world that are loosely connected with parts of their hard drives that are accessible to the public.
Internet Explorer	A Web browser created by Microsoft.
Internet Protocol	The "language of the Internet" that computers must "speak" in order to connect to one another and communicate with one another.
IP Number or Address	Like a zip code for a computer or server that is dedicated to the Internet. Every server has an IP address, but most also use a domain name, which is like a vanity license plate, to make it easier to remember the server's address to get to websites.
IRC	Internet relay chat. The Internet's version of live, real-time chatting.
ISDN	Integrated services digital network. A data connection that is much faster than a telephone line, able to transmit data at 128,000 bps versus 28,000 bps with a modem and phone line.
ISP	Internet service provider. A company that sets up a computer network to help you access the Internet and a more direct way to get online (like an onramp instead of a destination like a *COS*).
Kbps	Kilobits per second or thousands of bits per second. The speed of data over a phone or data line.
link	The way one website is connected to another on the

World Wide Web. Both text and images can be "programmed" to be a link to something else.

listserv   Special software to create an online forum about a topic where the posts or messages are broadcast into the email boxes of all of the subscribers to the list (instead of your going to a posting board to read the messages).

log in/log on   The act of accessing another computer; the process of your computer communicating with another and exchanging your account name and password to gain access.

lurk   To "hang out" in a chatroom or on a posting board without saying anything. It's appropriate to lurk for a while to see how the conversation goes, but lurking too long is considered rude. The person who lurks is called a "lurker."

mailing list   See *listserv*.

majordomo   Another special software that creates an Internet mailing list.

modem   A piece of hardware that acts as a communications device between your computer and another computer. Can be internal (within your computer) or external (a box that plugs into your computer).

MUDs   Multiuser dimensions. Computer network systems where many people log in and "inhabit a space," sometimes taking on different roles and acting out fantasy lives.

Net   Short name for the *Internet*.

netiquette   Net plus etiquette equals proper manners or mode of behavior online.

Netscape   The company that creates the popular Web browser Netscape Navigator, or "Netscape" for short.

network   With computers, a network is a system of connected computers either locally (within a company) or across a larger, external network like the Internet.

newsgroup   Also called Usenet newsgroup. An online forum on the Internet, like the posting boards on online services or on websites, usually topic-related.

online   On the Internet, connected.

peripherals	The additional hardware that you might connect to your computer such as a printer, a scanner, or a modem.
PGP	Pretty Good Privacy. A special software program that "encrypts" your data or puts a secret code around it so only someone with the "key" to the code can read it.
POP	Usually used to mean the "point of presence," which is the place a computer network connects so your *ISP* gets direct access to the Internet. Also used in email to mean "post office protocol" to arrange for your email program to retrieve your email from your host server. This information is obtained from your *ISP*.
post	*n.* a message on a posting board, newsgroup, or other forum; *v.* to put a message up or send a message to an online forum.
PPP	Point-to-point protocol. The newer standard for serial line Internet protocol. See *SLIP*.
protocol	A standard language or rules by which computers communicate with one another. Internet protocol is the rules computers follow to connect to one another on the Internet.
RAM	Random access memory. On your computer, RAM lets your computer run software (whereas the hard drive allows your computer to store software).
real time	Right now, as you read this, in the immediate present.
search engine	A type of searchable database at a website that uses a bot to search the Web for new websites, then indexes them so you can search for other sites in one place.
server	A computer that is dedicated to the Internet twenty-four hours a day, seven days a week, and that "serves up" data to the public by hosting websites and other databases.
shareware	Software available on the Internet on a trial basis until you pay the programmer who created it a small fee.
SLIP	Serial line Internet protocol. The original standard

"rules" to let your computer establish communication on the Internet using your modem and a phone line.

snail mail The nickname for mail sent the old-fashioned way—via the postal service.

software The intangible "stuff" that resides as programs and applications inside your computer. Once installed, they allow you to perform specific functions such as word processing or graphic layout.

spam The act of sending out repetitive, annoying, and off-topic posts to online forums. Considered bad manners or bad netiquette and can result in getting you flamed.

sysop Systems operator. Also known as a host (a person, not a computer). Someone who monitors and moderates a forum or a network.

T1 connection A very, very fast data-line connection, mostly used by big companies (1,544,000 bits per second is pretty darn fast!).

TCP/IP Transmission control protocol/Internet protocol. The standard set of rules that is the basis of all Internet communications and transferring of data.

telnet Internet software tool that gives you a remote way of accessing other computers via modem.

URL Uniform resource locator or Web address for a website.

virtual Not real, but "almost" real, nearly real. Virtual reality is simulated reality on the computer with three-dimensional graphics to make you think of "space" and location.

virus An annoying, sometimes destructive, software program that gets onto your computer's hard drive by installing corrupted store-bought software onto your computer, sharing floppy disks, or downloading unknown files from the Internet. Make sure you install computer virus protection software on your computer when you first buy it.

Web browser Also called a browser. Software used to view the World Wide Web. The most popular Web browsers

are Microsoft's Internet Explorer and Netscape's
Navigator.

website   A database of information on the World Wide Web
that incorporates graphics, sound, and video files
with text files.

wired   A slang term for being connected to the Internet.

World Wide
Web   The multimedia, interactive part of the Internet
linking text with sounds, graphics, video, animation,
and more.

Domain Name Suffixes

This list is subject to being expanded or changed and it is by no means complete.

.com	commercial entity or company
.edu	educational institution
.org	nonprofit organization
.mil	military
.gov	government

For a more complete list of country codes, go to
http://www.ics.uci.edu/pub/websoft/wwwstat/country-codes.txt

.au	Australia
.ca	Canada
.cn	China
.dk	Denmark
.fi	Finland
.fr	France
.de	Germany
.hk	Hong Kong
.is	Iceland
.in	India
.il	Israel
.it	Italy
.jp	Japan
.mx	Mexico
.nz	New Zealand
.ru	Russia
.sg	Singapore
.za	South Africa
.es	Spain
.se	Sweden
.ch	Switzerland
.th	Thailand
.tk	Turkey

Bibliography

Girl- and Women-Related Internet Books

For Young Girls
The Adventures of Tech Girl by Girl Tech (Foster City, CA: IDG Books, 1997)

Not for Young Girls
NetChick: A Smart-Girl Guide to the Wired World by Carla Sinclair (New York: Henry Holt, 1996)

Surfergrrls: Look, Ethel, Finally an Internet Book for Us by Laurel Gilbert and Crystal Kile (Seattle: Seal Press, 1996)

Wired Women: Gender and New Realities in Cyberspace by Lynn Cherny and Elizabeth Reba Weise (Seattle: Seal Press, 1996)

The Women's Guide to Online Services by Judith Broadhurst (New York: McGraw-Hill Publishing, 1995)

Women's Wire Web Directory by Ellen Pack (New York: Macmillan Computer Publishing, 1997)

Internet and Web-Related Magazines (the Paper Kind)

Internet World. For the more advanced Internet user, geared toward business online.

The Net. A good, mid-level magazine with beginner's tips and information for the savvy user, too. Check out the "Blue Pages" in the back of each issue with website reviews.

Online Access. A relatively easy-to-understand magazine about the Internet and the Web.

PC Novice's Internet Issues. PC Novice has magazines for the beginner computer user written in plain English. Look out for the occasional Internet issue.

The Web. Very entertainment-oriented with references to Web-based information and events pertaining to celebrities, television, movies, and more.

Wired. For the real technophile. Tends to be hard on the eyes (wild colors and graphics) but has provocative articles about technology issues.

URL INDEX

Activists

Kathy Watkins' Activist's Oasis   http://www.matisse.net/~kathy/activist/activist.html

Artists and Writers

Keri Advocat, photographer   http://www.snob.net/photo/index.html

Veronica Arnold, watercolorist
http://www.globalserve.net/~varnold

Jane Bynum, a graphic designer   http://www.grafika.com/

Beatrice R. Gilliam
http://GILLIB01@MSUMUSIK.MURSUKY.EDU

Jeanna Gollihur, "cyber poet"   http://www.baileygrp.com/life

"My Adventures on the Web" by Elana Lindquist
http://www.execpc.com/~elanal/My_Adventures.html

Xander Mellish, short stories and cartoons   http://www.xmel.com/

The Oldest Woman on the Web, by Sherry Miller
http://www.sherryart.com/sherry/columns/oldest.html

Karen Peeters, hat designer   http://www.club.innet.be/~ind1028

Almita Ranstrom's, art gallery
http://www.vashonisland.com/almitasgallery

Toshi's Web Journal
http://www.itp.tsoa.nyu.edu/~student/toshi/diary.html

Lesa Whyte's Redrum Coffeehouse
http://www.gothitica.com/redrum

Business

FedEx	http://www.fedex.com/
Field of Dreams	http://www.fodreams.com
Fortune	http://www.fortune.com/
Home Office Computing	http://www.hoc.com/
Hoover's Reference	http://www.hoovers.com/
Ideacafe	http://www.infocafe.com/
Inc.	http://www.inc.com/

Jane Applegate   http://www.janeapplegate.com
Small Business Administration http://www.sbaonline.sba.gov/
Small Business Adviser   http://www.isquare.com
Success   http://www.successmagazine.com/
UPS   http://www.ups.com/
Women's Connection   http://www.womenconnect.com/
Working Solo   http://www.workingsolo.com/

Career

Career Mosaic   http://www.careermosaic.com/
CareerPath   http://www.careerpath.com/
Cool Jobs   http://www.cooljobs.com/
Monster Board   http://www.monsterboard.com
Webgrrls   http://www.webgrrls.com/

Commercial Online Services

America Online   http://www.aol.com/
CompuServe   http://www.compuserve.com/
The Microsoft Network   http://www.msn.com/
Prodigy   http://www.prodigy.com/

Communications Software

HyperTerminal http://www.patelco.org/hyperterminal. html
MicroPhone Pro http://www.eu.intercon.com/products/mpwin.html
ProComm Plus
      http://www.datastorm.com/qdeck/products/procomm95/
WinComm   http://www.delrina.com

Communities

Echo   http://www.echonyc.com
Electric Minds   http://www.minds.com/
Folks Online   http://www.folksonline.com/
The WELL   http://www.well.com
Tripod   http://www.tripod.com

Education and Learning

American Association of University Women

http://www.aauw.org/

Artemis Guide to Women's Studies Programs in the U.S.

http://www.interport.net/~kater/

Feminist Fairytales   http://www.wp.com/dragontree/fairy.html

Homeschooling   http://www.kaleidoscapes.com/

UMBC Women's Studies website   http://www.umbc.edu/wmst/

Women's History in Archival Collections

http://www.utsa.edu/Library/Archives/links.htm.

Entertainment

Eonline   http://www.eonline.com/
Girls On Film   http://www.girlsonfilm.com/
Hollywood Online   http://www.hollywood.com/
Internet Movie Database   http://www.imdb.com/
Ladyslipper.org   http://www.ladyslipper.org/
Lifetime TV   http://www.lifetimetv.com/
Movielink   http://www.movielink.com/
Mr. Showbiz   http://www.mrshowbiz.com/
Musicgrrl   http://www.musicgrrl.com/
Rosie O'Donnell Show   http://www.rosieo.com/
Sloane   http://www.webgate.netl/~maenon/sloan
Sue Grafton   http://www.suegrafton.com
Sundance Institute   http://www.sundance.org/

Email Programs

Elm   http://www.myxa.com/elm.html
Eudora   http://ftp.qualcomm.com/ and http://www.eudora.com/
Pine   http://www.washington.edu/pine/

Family

Family.com   http://www.family.com/
Interactive Pregnancy Calendar   http://www.olen.com/baby/

Pampers	http://www.pampers.com
ParentSoup	http://www.parentsoup.com/
ParentTime	http://www.parenttime.com/

Finance

EDGAR	http://www.sec.gov/edgarhp.htm
eQuote	http://www.equote.com/
Fidelity Investments	http://www.fid-inv.com/
FinanceNet	http://www.financenet.gov/
Merrill Lynch	http://www.ml.com/
Money magazine	http://www.money.com/
New York Stock Exchange	http://www.nyse.com/
Quicken Financial Network	http://www.qfn.com/
Wall Street Journal	http://www.wsj.com/
WallStreet.net	http://www.wallstreet.net.

Food

American Dietetic Association	http://www.eatright.org/
eGG	http://www.foodwine.com/food/egg/
Epicurious Food	http://food.epicurious.com/
Yummyzine	http://www.yummyzine.com/

FTP Software

Fetch (for Macs)	http://www.shadowmac.org/pub/mirrors/ info-mac/_ Internet/fetch-302b2.hqx
WinFTP (for PCs)	http://www.winsite.com/info/ pc/win3/programr/winftp.zip/

Girl-Friendly Sites

American Girl	http://www.americangirl.com/
Bodyshock	http://www.bodyshock.com/
Girl Power	http://www.girlpower.com/
Girls Incorporated	http://www.girlsinc.org/
Girlspace	http://www.kotex.com
Kristi Yamaguchi	http://www.kristi.org

New Moon   http://www.newmoon.org/
Tara Lipinski   http://www.taralipinski.com/
TeenSpeak   http://www.teenspeak.com/
T-Room   http://www.troom.com/

Girls' Sites

Eleanor, 15   http://www.dragonfire.net/~grapecb/Eleanor/
Jeni, 16   http://macatawa.org/~jeni/
Katherine Torski, 12, and Her Dad   http://www.eci.com/torski/
Mary, 13   http://embers.aol.com/hov/index4.html

Good Causes

The Body (AIDS)   http://www.thebody.org/
Cancercare   http://www.cancercare.org/
Envirolink (Environment)   http://envirolink.org/
Foundation Center   http://fdncenter.org/
Girls Incorporated   http://www.girlsinc.org/
Impact Online   http://www.impactonline.org/
Internet Nonprofit Center   http://www.nonprofit.org/

Gopher Software

HGopher (for PCs)
      http://www.winsite.com/info/pc/win3/winsock/ hgoph24.zip/
Turbo Gopher (for Macs)
                http://www.shadowmac.org/pub/mirrors/
                info-mac/_Internet/turbo-gopher-203.hqx

Health/Medical

Albert Einstein College of Medicine   http://www.aecom.yu.edu/
Alzheimer Canada   http://www.alzheimer.ca
Anatomy of the Hand and Carpal Tunnel
                http://www.scoi.com/handanat.htm
Avon's Breast Cancer Awareness Crusade Online
                http://www.avoncrusade.com/

Caregiver Network   http://www.caregiver.on.ca
Columbia Presbyterian   http://cpmcnet.columbia.edu/
Healthy Ideas   http://www.healthyideas.com/
Healthy Woman   http://www.healthgate.com/
Mayo Clinic   http://www.mayo.edu/
National Alliance of Breast Cancer Organizations
                        http://www.nabco.org/
National MS Society   http://www.nmss.org/
National MS Society, N.Y. http://www.msnyc.org/
Planned Parenthood Federation http://www.ppfa.org/
Prevention's Healthy Ideas   http://www.healthyideas.com
Rare Genetic Diseases in Children Life-Link Topic Board
        http://mcrc4.med.nyu.edu/~murphp01/brdmenu3.htm
Repetitive Strain Injury Page
              http://www.engr.unl.edu/ee/eeshop/rsi.html
WEBster: Ergonomics and Computer Injuries
             http://lucky.innet.com/~kathiw/ergo.html

Hobbies

Garden Escape Chat Room   http://www.garden.com/
Gardening   http://www.gardening.com/
Home Improvement   http://www.homeideas.com/
Journal of Online Genealogy   http://www.onlinegenealogy.com/
Virtual Florist   http://www.virtualflorist.com/

Internet Browsers

Microsoft Internet Explorer
             http://www.microsoft.com/ie/default.asp
Netscape Navigator   http://www.netscape.com/

Internet Relay Chat (IRC) Server

Undernet   http://www.undernet.org/

Internet Relay Chat (IRC) Software

Homer (for Macs)	http://www.shadowmac.org/pub/mirrors/ infomac/_ Internet/homer-094.hqx
Ircle (for Macs)	http://www.shadowmac.org/pub/mirrors/ info-mac/_ Internet/ircle-25.hqx
mIRC (for PCs)	http://www.mirc.com/

Internet Service Providers

Boston: TIAC	http://www.tiac.com/
Chicago: EnterAct	http://www.enteract.com/
Denver: SuperNet	http://www.csn.net/
Maine: cyberTours	http://www.cybertours.com/cybertours/home.html
Miami: Florida Internet	http://www.flinet.com/main.html
New York City: Interport	http://www.interport.net/
New York City: Panix	http://www.panix.com/
Orlando: Florida Internet	http://www.flinet.com/main.html
Philadelphia: LibertyNet	http://www.libertynet.com/
Pittsburgh: Westmoreland Online	http://www.westol.com/
San Francisco: Best	http://www.best.com/
San Francisco: Sirius	http://www.sirius.com/
Texas: HubNet	http://www.hub.ofthe.net/

ISP Reviews

CNET's reviews of local ISPs

http://www.cnet.com/Content/Reviews/Compare/ISP/

Motherhood

Interactive pregnancy calendar	http://www.olen.com/baby
La Leche League (by Sue Anne Kendell)	http://www.lalecheleague.org

Sue Anne Kendall, who has resources about breastfeeding
>
> http://www.prairienet.org/~sak

Yummyzine   http://www.yummyzine.com

News

Allpolitics   http://allpolitics.com/
CNN   http://www.cnn.com/
Wall Street Journal Interactive   http://www.wsj.com/

Newsgroup Software

Newswatcher (for Mac)
>
> http://www.shadowmac.org/pub/mirrors/
> info-mac/_ Internet/newswatcher-216.hqx

Trumpet NNTP Newsreader (for PC)
>
> http://www.winsite.com/info/pc/win3/util/wtpkt10a.zip/

Parental Control Sites

Cyber Patrol   http://www.microsys.com/cyber/
CYBERsitter   http://www.solidoak.com/
Cyber Snoop   pearlsw.com/csnoop/snoop.htm
Net Nanny   http://www.netnanny.com/
RatedPG   http://www.ratedpg.com/
SafeSearch   http://www.safesearch.com/
Surf Watch   http://www.surfwatch.com/
The Internet Filter   http://www.turnercom.com/
X-Stop   http://www.xstop.com/

Personal Websites

Veronica Arnold, watercolor gallery
>
> http://www.globalserve.net/~varnold

Anne Baker   http://members.tripod.com/~Stasia/index.html
Science teacher's website, by Laura Bashlor
>
> http://www.gatecom.com/~lauralou

Wendy Bumgardner's Volksmarch and Walking Index
                    http://www.teleport.com/~walking/
Charley Buntrock   http://pubweb.nwu.edu/~cjb168
Jane Bynum, a graphic designer http://www.grafika.com/
Celestial Circle   http://www.geocities.com/Athens/5224.
Lutgarde Gaddum-Mees   http://www.tornado.be/~gaddum/
Beatrice R. Gilliam
              http://GILLIB01@MSUMUSIK.MURSUKY.EDU
Jeanna Gollihur's "cyber poems"
                    http://www.baileygrp.com/life
Molly Gordon, artist, PR person, and coach
                    http://www.halcyon.com/molly
Marva Jackson's business site
          http://www.konekshuns.com/marvalous_konekshuns.html
Kathryn Koromilas
          http://www.geocities.com/Athens/Acropolis/1969/
          room.htm and http://www.zip.com.au/~kk/kjhome.htm
Christine Kossman for her son who is gay
                    http://www.i2.i-2000.com/~ckossman
Kathleen Lange, a pediatric nurse practitioner
                    http://weber.u.washington.edu/~klange
"My Adventures on the Web," by Elana Lindquist
            http://www.execpc.com/~elanal/My_Adventures.html
Xander Mellish, short stories and cartoons
                    http://www.xmel.com/
The Oldest Woman on the Web, by Sherry Miller
            http://www.sherryart.com/sherry/columns/oldest.html
Karen Peeters, hat designs   http://www.club.innet.be/~ind1028
Almita Ranstrom   http://www.vashonisland.com/almitasgallery
Wagner High School, Clark Air Force Base
                    http://www.whoa.org/
Lesa Whyte's Redrum Coffeehouse
                    http://www.gothitica.com/redrum/

Pioneers

Stephanie Brail   http://www.amazoncity.com/
Susan Defife   http://www.womenconnect.com
Amy Goodloe   http://www.women-online.com
Stacy Horn   http://www.echonyc.com/

Joan Korenman	http://www.umbc.edu/wmst/
Ellen Pack	http://www.women.com/
Nancy Rhine	http://www.digitalcities.com/
Eva Shaderowfsky	http://www.webgrrls.com/eva/

Publications

GeekGirl	http://www.geekgirl.com.au/geekgirl/
gURL	http://www.gurl.com/
Maximag	http://www.maximag.com/
NrrdGrrl	http://www.nrrdgrrl.com/
Papermag	http://www.papermag.com
Wired	http://www.wired.com
Women's Wire	http://www.women.com/
WomenZone	http://www.womenzone.com/

Relationships

American Bridal Registry	http://www.abregistry.com/
BridalNet	http://www.bridalnet.com
Internet Wedding Links Global Search FIND Page	
	http://netdreams.com/awedding/search.html
The Knot	http://www.theknot.com/
Match.com	http://www.match.com/
Plan A Wedding	http://www.planawedding.com/form.html
Swoon	http://www.swoon.com
Way Cool Weddings	http://www.waycoolweddings.com

Research Resources

| E-Library | http://www.elibrary.com/ |

Search Engines

AltaVista	http://www.altavista.digital.com/
Excite	http://www.excite.com/
Femina	http://www.femina.com/
Infoseek	http://www.infoseek.com/

Lycos   http://www.lycos.com/
Yahoo   http://www.yahoo.com/

Seniors

Administration on Aging
                    http://www.aoa.dhhs.gov/aoa/pages/jpostlst.html
American Association of Retired Persons   http://www.aarp.org/
America's Guide: Retirement Living and Senior Care
                    http://www.americasguide.com/index.html/
Eldercare Website   http://www.elderweb.com/index.html
RetireNet   http://www.retire.net/
SeniorCom   http://www.senior.com/
SeniorNet   http://www.seniornet.com

Shopping/Products

1-800-Flowers   http://www.1800flowers.com/
Amazon.com   http://www.amazon.com/
Autobytel   http://www.autobytel.com
Aveda   http://www.aveda.com/
Avon   http://www.avon.com/
Barnes & Noble   http://www.barnesandnoble.com/
Bookstacks Unlimited   http://www.books.com/
CD Now   http://www.cdnow.com/
Clinique   http://www.clinique.com/
Godiva Chocolates   http://www.godiva.com/
J. Crew   http://www.jcrew.com/
Ladyslipper, for music   http://www.ladyslipper.org/
Lands' End   http://www.landsend.com/
Lee Jeans   http://www.leejeans.com
MusicBoulevard   http://www.musicboulevard.com
The Music Spot   http://www.musicspot.com/
Spiegel   http://www.spiegel.com/
Tide   http://www.tide.com/

Shopping for Computers

CompUSA   http://www.compusa.com/
Computer City   http://www.computercity.com/main.html

Cyberian Outpost   http://www.cybout.com/cyberian.html
Gateway 2000   http://www.gateway2000.com/
IBM Consumer Division   http://www.pc.ibm.com/
Internet Shopping Network http://www.isn.com/
MacWarehouse catalog
                http://www.warehouse.com/macwarehouse/
Micron   http://www.micron.com/
MicroWarehouse catalog
                http://www.warehouse.com/microwarehouse/
Power Computing   http://www.pc.ibm.com/

Software

Filemine   http://www.filemine.com/
Jumbo   http://www.jumbo.com/
Shareware.com   http://www.shareware.com/
ZDNet Software Library   http://www.hotfiles.com/

Sports

GolfWeb   http://www.golfweb.com/
Just Sports for Women http://www.justwomen.com/contents.html
Volksmarch and Walking Index
                http://www.teleport.com/~walking/
Women in Sports   http://www.makeithappen.com/wis/
Women's Sports   http://CNNSI.com/womens/

Taxes

IRS Electronic-Filing System
            http://www.irs.ustreas.gov/plain/elec_svs/ol-txpyr.html
Tax Site Directory   http://www.taxsites.com/
TurboTax Center   http://www.intuit.com/turbotax/

Technology News

CNET   http://cnet.com/
News.com   http://www.news.com/

TechWeb   http://www.techweb.com/
Wired.com   http://www.wired.com/
ZDNet   http://www.zdnet.com/

Travel

Adventure Travel Site for Women
      http://www.gorge.net/business/adventure/women/
American Airlines   http://www.american-air.com
Epicurious   http://www.travel.epicurious.com/
Executive Women's Travel Network
      http://www.delta-air.com/womenexecs
GORP   http://www.gorp.com/
Holiday Inn   http://www.holidayinn.com/
Internet Guide to Hostelling   http://www.hostels.com/
Internet Travel Network   http://www.itn.net/
Latin World   http://www.latinworld.com
Lonely Planet Online   http://www.lonelyplanet.com/
Ramada   http://www.ramada.com/
Simple Traveler   http://www.simpletraveler.com/
South American Explorers Club   http://www.samexplo.org/
Travelgrrl   http://www.travelgrrl.com/
Travelocity   http://www.travelocity.com/
USAir   http://www.usairways.com/

Virus Protection Software

Disinfectant
      http://ciac.llnl.gov/ciac/ToolsMacVirus.html#Disinfectant
Norton Utilities   http://www.symantec.com/cgi-bin/menu.cgi
SAM   http://ciac.llnl.gov/ciac/ToolsMacVirus.html#SAM

Weather

FAA   http://www.faa.gov/
National Weather Service   http://www.nws.noaa.gov/
Weather Channel online   http://www.weather.com

Web Resources

Country Codes
http://www.ics.uci.edu/pub/websoft/wwwstat/country-codes.txt
Geocities   http://www.geocities.com/
Hitchhiker's Guide to the Internet
http://www.cis.ohio-state.edu/htbin/rfc/rfc1118.html
The List   http://www.thelist.com/
List of Gender-Related Mailing Lists
http://research.umbc.edu/~korenman/wmst/forums.html
List of Newsgroups
http://www.cis.ohio-state.edu:80/hypertext/faq/usenet/
Liszt   http://www.liszt.com/
NetGuide   http://www.netguide.com/
New Internet User FAQ
http://www.cis.ohio-state.edu/htbin/rfc/rfc1206.html
Pierre Violet's List of Smileys
http://www.netsurf.org/~violet/Smileys/
Zen and the Art of the Internet
http://www.itec.suny.edu/SUNY/DOC/internet/zen.html

Women's Resources

Amazoncity   http://www.amazoncity.com
Artemis   http://www.interport.net/~kater
Beatrice's Web Guide   http://www.bguide.com
California Abortion and Reproductive Rights Action League
http://www.caral.org/
Cybergrrl Village   http://village.cybergrrl.com
Cybergrrl Webstation   http://www.cybergrrl.com/
Femina   http://www.femina.com/
Feminist Activist Resources
http://www.clark.net/pub/s-gray/feminist.html
Feminist.com   http://www.feminist.com/
Feminist Majority   http://www.feminist.org
HomeArts   http://www.homearts.com
WWWomen   http://www.wwwomen.com/
MondoGirl   http://www.mondogirl.com

Webgrrls: Ft. Lauderdale, FL
                             http://www.webgrrls.com/ftlauderdale/
Webgrrls: Germany   http://www.webgrrls.de/
Webgrrls: Hawaii   http://www.webgrrls.com/hawaii/
Webgrrls: Hong Kong   http://www.webgrrls.com/hk/
Webgrrls: Houston, TX   http://www.freshpages.com/webgrrls/
Webgrrls: Ithaca, NY   http://www.webgrrls.com/ithaca/
Webgrrls: Jacksonville, FL   http://www.jaxflorida.com/webgrrls
Webgrrls: Ketchikan, Alas.
                   http://puffin.ptlalaska.net/~jgoforth/wgindex.html
Webgrrls: London, Ontario (Forest City)
                        http://www.info.london.on.ca/webgrrls/
Webgrrls: Long Island, N.Y.   http://www.bworks.com/wgli
Webgrrls: Los Angeles, Calif.   http://www.webgrrls.com/la/
Webgrrls: Melbourne, Australia
                  http://www.home.aone.net.au/webgrrls/
Webgrrls: Milan, Italy   http://www.italynet.com/webgrrls/
Webgrrls: Minneapolis/St. Paul, Minn.
                           http://www.webgrrls.com/tc/
Webgrrls: Mississauga, Ontario http://www.webgrrls.com/mssauga/
Webgrrls: Montreal, Quebec   http://www.webgrrls.com/montreal/
Webgrrls: Netherlands   http://www.mediaport.org/~webgrrls/
Webgrrls: New York City
                      http://www.webgrrls.com/ny/index.html
Webgrrls: Niagara Region, Ontario
                      http://www.webgrrls.niagara.com/
Webgrrls: Oklahoma City, OK   http://webgrrls.com/okcity/
Webgrrls: Ottawa, Ontario   http://www.webgrrls.com/ottawa/
Webgrrls: Raleigh/Durham/Chapel Hill, N.C. (Triangle)
                      http://www.trianglewebgrrls.com/
Webgrrls: Sacramento, Calif.
                   http://www.webgrrls.com/sacramento/
Webgrrls: San Diego, Calif.   http://www.webgrrls.com/sandiego/
Webgrrls: San Francisco, Calif. http://www.webgrrls.com/sf/
Webgrrls: Seattle, Wash.   http://www.ixa.net/~grrl/
Webgrrls: Silicon Valley, Calif. http://www.webgrrls.com/sv/
Webgrrls: Southeastern Wisconsin
                   http://www.webgrrls.com/sewisconsin/
Webgrrls: Space Coast, Fla. http://www.webgrrls.com/spacecoast/
Webgrrls: Sydney, Australia   http://www.webgrrls.com/sydney/

INDEX

ABOUT THE AUTHOR

Aliza Sherman is a writer and Web adventurer living in New York City and commuting daily to cyberspace. She is president of her own company, Cybergrrl, and founder of Webgrrls International. In her spare time, she answers email. Her email address is aps@cgim.com.